GATEWAY SERIES IN EDUCATIONAL PSYCHOLOGY

BRYCE B. HUDGINS, EDITOR

WASHINGTON UNIVERSITY

F. E. PEACOCK PUBLISHERS, INC.

MEASUREMENT AND EVALUATION

FREDERICK G. BROWN

IOWA STATE UNIVERSITY

To Jeffrey, Kirk and Danny

CONTENTS

FOREWORD

Those of us who teach courses in educational psychology are aware of the difficulties entailed in providing students with text materials of sufficient breadth to encompass and reflect the issues and problems of this growing field of study and practice. The Gateway Series in Educational Psychology is an effort to span the area without sacrificing depth of treatment as often happens in introductory or survey courses. Each of the basic books in the series deals with one of the major topics that define educational psychology today, and each is written by an author who has specialized in that topic. The series will offer a second kind of book that will ordinarily treat a more limited topic or subfield. These satellite volumes will also be written with the beginning student in mind.

Measurement and Evaluation by Professor Frederick G. Brown is the first volume to appear in the Gateway Series. Professor Brown has conducted original work in the field of measurement, and he has extensive practical experience gained in designing testing programs, and in teaching courses in psychological tests and measurements. In this book he has presented the fundamental concepts of measurement and evaluation in a perspective that should make them readily comprehensible, and at the same time demonstrate to the prospective or practicing teacher how such concepts are relevant to the tasks of educators. He has achieved the difficult objective of teaching his subject in a nontechnical way without distorting its substance.

BRYCE B. HUDGINS
Editor

PREFACE

Perhaps no topic is more misunderstood by teachers, both practicing and prospective, than the role of testing in education. The reasons are several. We have all been exposed to tests for so many years, and in so many forms, that we have formed strong opinions about their value; these opinions interfere with an objective consideration of the values of testing. Furthermore, many teachers, who rightfully see their goal as helping children to learn and develop, feel that any evaluation hinders the attainment of this goal. And the discussion of evaluation and measurement usually is only a subsidiary part of the teacher education curriculum and is not viewed as the most exciting nor relevant aspect of a teacher's preparation. In short, testing is often seen only as a necessary evil.

The goal of this book is to illustrate how tests, and other measuring instruments, can further the educational process—how they can be used in planning, conducting and evaluating instruction. While we will stress the advantages of tests, hopefully we have also been honest about their limitations.

The book was written primarily for an introductory course in educational psychology. Thus those aspects of measurement and evaluation which are most pertinent to the classroom teacher are emphasized. Several chapters are devoted to classroom tests and other measures of achievement with less space given to ability and personality tests. Technical considerations, especially statistics, have been limited to the minimal amount needed in order to understand the basic concepts. We have emphasized the interpretation of the various types of scores rather than their computation. And we have included chapters on grading and the evaluation of instruction.

This book is a text, not a "how-to-do-it" manual. While we have included numerous examples and some suggestions for projects, the discussion will be more meaningful if supplemented by demonstrations of testing procedures, detailed examination of tests and test manuals, practice in item writing, and analysis of test scores and items. A text is but an introduction; thorough understanding will come only with experience in constructing, administering and interpreting tests in "real-life" situations.

Especial thanks are owed to Mrs. Judy Dodds, who not only typed the manuscript but made many valuable suggestions, and to my fellow members of our Palo Alto evening seminar—Bob Gowin, Bryce Hudgins, David Madsen, Jonas Soltis, Ira Steinberg and Roger Wilk—who stimulated my interest in educational problems and encouraged me to write this book.

1

THE FUNCTIONS OF TESTING IN EDUCATION

Testing, testing, testing—several years ago a group of school administrators published a report with this title (Joint Committee on Testing, 1962). Although the focus of the report was on testing programs external to the schools—particularly college admissions and scholarship testing programs—the choice of title reflects a concern with the possible overuse of tests in education. Yet within this same report another statement is made: To teach without testing is unthinkable.

Probably anyone connected with education—be he teacher, administrator, or student—has at some time felt that the educational process consisted of one test followed by another. And there is no doubt that a very large number of tests is administered in schools each year. One source (Mehrens and Lehmann, 1969) estimates that approximately 200 million standardized tests are sold each year. This count does not include any of the teacher-made tests which are given in classrooms throughout the country every school day. Although the exact number of classroom (teacher-made) tests administered is not known and probably never will be, there is no doubt but that it is many times the number of standardized tests administered each year. If we assume that four teacher-made tests are administered for every standardized test, certainly an exceedingly conservative estimate, we are talking about a billion tests per year!

But what are all these tests used for? What are they attempting to measure? How successful are they? How do we know if a test successfully fulfills its function? What are the characteristics of a good test? Are tests fair indices, or are they biased? Are tests being used where they should not be used? Conversely, are there situations where tests are not used but where they might prove valuable? In the following pages we will attempt to answer these, and other, questions regarding the use of tests in education.

AN APPROACH TO TESTING IN EDUCATION

Our concern in this book is with testing in education. And, as the primary concern of education is with learning—learning specific bits of knowledge, learning problem-solving skills, learning about oneself and other people, learning how to develop values— an appropriate place to begin our study is by considering how testing can facilitate the learning process. As a framework for our discussion, we will consider a series of questions.

First, *what is the student's present level of developed abilities, skills, knowledge, and personality characteristics?* In short, what sort of person are we trying to teach? The importance of this question is obvious; effective teaching (and learning) involves taking a student at his present level of development and guiding him to a higher level. To do this, we must know his current developmental level on the skill in question. It is equally obvious that developmental status often can be assessed by psychological tests. This is not to say that tests are the only way to obtain this information (estimates of intellectual development may be obtained from tests or from teacher's judgments) or that all pertinent information can be obtained from tests (there is no good test of academic motivation available) but rather that tests can often provide valuable information.

We also should emphasize that we are talking about both very broad abilities and quite narrow skills. For example, before enrolling a student in a physics course we might want to know something about his general level of intellectual ability, his numerical and abstract reasoning ability (or aptitude, if you wish), his background in specific prerequisite mathematics courses, and even his current knowledge of physics per se.

In essence we are asking: *What are the implications of the student's skills and characteristics for appropriate placement in the instructional sequence?* One of the aphorisms of education is that we should teach the child, not the subject; that is, education should be individualized. Of course, the economics and logistics of most educational settings do not allow for completely individualized instruction. Yet in most situations, several alternative instructional approaches are available. The question then becomes: Which approach is optimal for a given student? Here data on student characteristics become relevant, as it is likely that certain types of students will profit from different approaches.

The alert reader will realize that a prior consideration is involved. To optimally assign students to instructional treatments presupposes knowledge of which approach is optimal for each student. Although experience and logic may provide some aid, the best guide is research showing what types of students learn best under each alternative method. Such research is rarely available. However, ideally the results of such research would be used to determine an individual's placement within alternative approaches.

Given that the student has embarked upon a given unit or course of study, the next question is: *How is his learning progressing?* The concern here is with monitoring learning. In the ideal case, such as in certain computer-aided instructional systems, monitoring is continuous and a record of every response the student makes is available. Near the other extreme, the typical classroom procedure is to monitor students' learning (that is, test the students) only at the end of a unit or lesson.

The purpose of monitoring students' progress is not just to provide the instructor with some evidence of each student's rate of progress. A more important purpose is to provide students with evidence of the effectiveness of their learning. In the typical instructional program the student is presented with some stimulus material; on the basis of his previous learning he makes a response. Monitoring provides him with feedback regarding the accuracy of his response—that is, provides him with information regarding the progress of his learning. The reader who has studied the psychology of learning will also realize that, as learning is more efficient with immediate feedback and performance does not improve without any feedback, immediate feedback as to the accuracy of a response should lead to more effective learning.

We can take our analysis one step further. If education is to be truly individualized and based on previous learning, then continuous monitoring should also provide the basis for determining the course of future instruction and even altering present plans, depending on the student's progress in the early stages of instruction. That is, one pattern of responses in the early stages of learning will lead to one treatment, a different pattern of responses will lead to different instructional material.

At the end of an instructional sequence we ask a fourth question: *Has the student mastered the material or skill being taught?* If the material being taught is capable of being broken down into specific skills, and if the development of the topic is sequential, then the answer to this question is implicit in the previous question. However, if the skill being taught supersedes any individual part, or if the material is presented in other than a tightly organized cumulative sequence, a test of mastery is appropriate. The typical end-of-unit classroom exam is, of course, designed to serve this function.

Also implicit in this question is the assumption that the desired outcomes or objectives of the instructional program can be specified. Although this requirement may seem obvious, the reader should not have much trouble thinking of a course that he has taken where the objectives were not clearly specified or were given in such general terms (e.g., to learn the fundamentals of chemistry, to learn to speak French, to teach an appreciation of classical music) as to be essentially meaningless. The specification of objectives, in fact, is one of the most difficult aspects of education, and we will return to this problem repeatedly throughout the book.

But in education we are not interested only in the immediate outcomes of a given segment of instruction. We are also interested in questions such as: *Has the material learned been retained over longer periods of time? Can the skills learned be transferred to new situations and problems? Can the material learned be integrated with learnings from other experiences?* It is obvious that tests can also help us answer these questions.

The approach is outlined in Figure 1.1.

An Example

The approach discussed in the previous pages can be illustrated by an example. Suppose that a junior high school offers two math sequences in eighth grade; those students with more mathematical aptitude and ability can go directly into algebra, while the remaining students take an additional year of general mathematics fol-

FIGURE 1.1
FLOWCHART ILLUSTRATING AN APPROACH TO TESTING IN EDUCATION

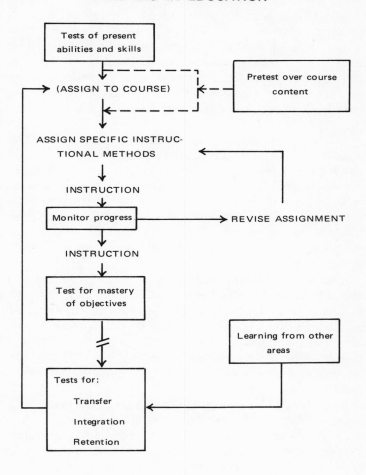

lowed by algebra in ninth grade. The problem is to determine which students will benefit from taking algebra in eighth grade.

According to our model, the first step is to determine the mathematical aptitude, abilities, and skills of the seventh-grade students. Here various lines of evidence may be available for each student: current and past mathematics grades, scores on the mathematics (or arithmetic) sections of the yearly achievement battery, teachers' recommendations, measures of general academic ability. To these, let us add one other, a test designed specifically to measure aptitude for algebra. On the basis of the performance on these measures, we select[1] enough students to fill one section of the algebra class and assign the remainder to the regular eighth-grade mathematics program.

Let us now be concerned only with those students who take algebra in the eighth grade. At the beginning of the year, the instructor gives a pretest to determine what algebraic concepts the students are already familiar with, either intuitively or from previous study. The results of this test help the instructor plan his teaching.

As the course progresses, the instructor gives periodic assignments, quizzes, and unit examinations to check on students' learning. The results of these quizzes again help him plan his instruction —for example, he may find that certain processes or concepts are not well understood, and thus he must attempt to present them in another manner. The results may also suggest specific assignments for different students; for example, a student who is weak in factoring might be assigned additional problems to develop his skill in this area.

At the end of the course, a final exam is given to test students' mastery of the objectives of the course. Besides indicating whether the students have attained the objectives, this mastery test will provide an additional check on teaching effectiveness. It may also provide clues for improving the selection procedure; that is, if the characteristics of the students who did not do well in the course can be identified, the selection procedure can be changed to take these factors into account.

The crucial test, of course, is the long-range effects of the course. Scores on yearly achievement batteries and performance in subsequent math courses and courses in related fields (e.g., chemistry and physics) can provide information on the retention of the material and its integration with learning from other areas. The effect of the course on attitudes towards mathematics could also be ascertained, for example, by determining whether students in the

---

[1] There are various possible ways to select the students who will take algebra; the details of these procedures need not concern us here (see Brown, 1970, or Cronbach, 1970, for a fuller discussion). Ideally, selection would be based on procedures developed through previous research. Also, the number of students selected would depend on the proportion of students who will profit from early instruction in algebra and on practical constraints within the curriculum (e.g., availability of teachers). For illustrative purposes, we have used a situation where only one section of students will take algebra.

accelerated program elect more math courses in future years or enter curricula requiring strong mathematical backgrounds.

This example, like any example we might choose, does not illustrate all aspects of the approach outlined. It does, however, indicate some of the various roles that testing can and should play in the instructional process.

Prerequisites of the Approach

Certain basic prerequisites must be met if the approach described is to be utilized. The objectives of any given unit of instruction must be clearly specified and a sequence of instructional steps that will lead to the attainment of these objectives must be devised. In other words, we must precisely define what we want to teach and then develop methods to teach it. We must know at what developmental stage students can profit from studying different materials. Furthermore, we must provide alternative approaches for learning and have evidence as to which alternative is most effective for each type of individual. We must be able to continuously monitor each student's progress and to alter his instruction if the method he is assigned to proves ineffective. Finally, but perhaps easiest to attain, we must develop tests to measure the characteristics, outcomes, or skills that must be measured at various stages of instruction.

The preceding paragraph points out the weakness of the approach—except in rare cases, we do not currently have the educational theory, research, and technology, nor the financial resources, to implement such a program. We do not know, for example, what instructional methods are optimal for what type of students in the various subject areas. Nor, with the exception of certain computer-aided instructional systems (see, e.g., Atkinson, 1968; Glaser, 1968), do we have the facilities to continually monitor student performance. In most cases, course objectives are not clearly specified, nor have well-developed instructional methods for attaining these objectives been devised. (Programmed instruction perhaps comes closest to this goal.) In spite of decades of research on intellectual abilities, there is still little agreement on the basic intellectual skills, let alone knowledge of how they apply to learning. And so on.

Thus, in most educational settings, testing programs do not approach the comprehensiveness of the model described. At best we try to define our objectives and use evaluation devices to measure if these objectives have been attained at the end of a course. We recognize individual differences in learning ability by assigning students to different courses or tracks on the basis of their past grades, achievement test scores, and scores on scholastic aptitude or intelligence tests. We attempt to measure growth and transfer of learning through periodic (usually once a year) achievement batteries. In short, when viewed against a model testing program, current practices represent a dearth of testing, not an overabundance.

SOME BASIC DISTINCTIONS

Throughout the previous pages we have referred to testing in education; yet at no time did we define what was meant by "a test."

Test

A *test* has been defined as a systematic procedure for measuring a sample of an individual's behavior (Brown, 1970). Although this definition is purposely quite broad, it has several limiting aspects. Note, first, that a test is a systematic procedure. This requirement means that test items must be constructed following certain rules, that procedures for administering the test must be established, and that scoring procedures must be specified in detail. Most important of all, it means that all persons will take the same items under comparable conditions.

A test is also but a sample of behavior. Any test, however long, will include only a sample of all possible items; to the extent that it representatively samples the domain being measured, it will be an adequate test. A test also measures behavior; it requires the student to demonstrate, by a performance as simple as marking a space on an answer sheet or as complex as writing an essay, what he has learned. If, for some reason, an individual does not, or cannot, perform, we may misinterpret what he has learned.

We might also note what is not included in the definition. There is no requirement that a test take any particular format—for example, that it require use of paper and pencil. Nor is there any limitation on the content covered by tests—we can measure specific classroom learnings or broad personality traits. And, finally, there is no requirement that the person know that he is being tested nor that he make specific preparation for the testing. In fact, when testing young children, the test is usually structured as a game so the child will not be aware that he is being tested.

Measurement

Implicit in the definition is the idea that a test is a measuring instrument. The concept of *measurement* is very complex (see, e.g., Kerlinger, 1965, Chapter 23; Guilford, 1954, Chapter 1) but basically it is concerned with how much of a quality or characteristic an individual possesses. Although measurement can exist at various levels, in education we are primarily concerned with two of them. In some circumstances we merely want to rank persons in order; for example, we may want to select the 25 best math students out of 200 eighth graders for placement in an accelerated math sequence. To accomplish this we only need an instrument that ranks students on math ability; we do not need to know the (absolute) amount of math each student knows or how much better these 25 students are than the other students. Scales which rank individuals are called ordinal scales.

In other circumstances, particularly when we want to subject scores to statistical analyses, we would like a scale that not only ranks students but also provides information about the magnitude of differences between students. Thus test developers attempt to build scales which have equal-sized units. On these scales, called interval scales, a score difference of say, 5 points, means the same thing at different points on the scale.

Two further points about measurement are particularly relevant to our discussion. First, measurement is nonevaluative. When we measure something, such as a student's intelligence or ability in mathematics, we only indicate how much of the characteristic he possesses. The measurement process puts no value on the amount; any evaluation is added by the person interpreting the score. Second, measurement involves comparing an individual score to some scale or standard. In most educational and psychological measurement, the standard used is the performance of other students; that is, measurement is concerned with interindividual differences. Although having meaningful absolute standards would be of great value, such standards are not common in education. Rather we compare an individual to his peers and interpret his performance in comparison to the performance of his peers.

Although measurement, and consequently testing, is nonevaluative, test scores are frequently used when making judgments and evaluations about individual students. For example, the teacher must decide whether a student has learned enough to progress to the next instructional unit or even to the next grade. He must decide whether a particular teaching method or instruction approach is effective, either for the class as a whole or for an individual student. He must decide if a particular child is progressing in accord with his abilities. And so on.

All these circumstances require the teacher to make a judgment —to evaluate a student or approach. In each case, test scores may be of some aid in making the evaluation, but they will not tell the entire story. The evaluation process is broader than measurement, and the added dimension is the assigning of worth or value to the performance. In making an evaluation the teacher will consider data of various types and from various sources—his knowledge of the students, their background and experiences; the learning context; the community and school system; and his own values and biases. All of these factors will be weighed by the teacher (or other decision maker) and used to make an evaluation. In short, measurement is concerned with "how much"; evaluation with "how good."

Learning

Finally, we should distinguish between learning and measurement. The learning process involves the acquisition of knowledge and skills; measurement involves assessing the degree to which such knowledge and skills have been mastered. Thus although learning and measurement are related, they are not synonymous.

We mention this obvious distinction only to make one point— that measurement does not necessarily have to utilize the same processes as does learning. All measurement has to do is provide an accurate measure of the outcomes of learning. To illustrate, spelling ability might be assessed by test items which require the student to select the improperly spelled word in a list of words. This does not mean that the teaching of spelling must proceed in an analogous fashion or that the test would be invalid because it utilizes a process other than that used in the learning situation.

The usefulness of the test is a function of the accuracy with which it measures the desired outcome, not of its similarity to the learning process.

SUMMARY

In this chapter we have attempted to build a framework for discussing the use of tests in education. We did this by outlining an approach to testing in education. This approach considered five major areas: (1) the student's present level of developed skills, abilities, and characteristics; (2) the implications of these characteristics when selecting educational experiences; (3) the monitoring of learning progress; (4) measurement of mastery; and (5) measuring retention, transfer, and integration. In addition, we defined three fundamental terms—test, measurement, and evaluation—and discussed the relationship between measurement and evaluation and that between measurement and learning.

REFERENCES

ATKINSON, R. C. "Computerized Instruction and the Learning Process," *American Psychologist,* Vol. 23 (1968), pp. 225–39.

BROWN, F. G. *Principles of Educational and Psychological Testing.* Hinsdale, Ill.: The Dryden Press, 1970.

CRONBACH, L. J. *Essentials of Psychological Testing.* 3rd ed. New York: Harper & Row, Publishers, 1970.

GLASER, R. "Adapting the Elementary School Curriculum to Individual Performance," in *Proceedings of the 1967 Invitational Conference on Testing Problems,* pp. 3–36. Princeton, N.J.: Educational Testing Service, 1968.

GUILFORD, J. P. *Psychometric Methods.* 2nd ed. New York: McGraw-Hill Book Co., 1954.

JOINT COMMITTEE ON TESTING (American Association of School Administrators, Council of Chief State School Officers, and National Association of Secondary-School Principals). *Testing, Testing, Testing.* Washington, D.C., 1962.

KERLINGER, F. N. *Foundations of Behavioral Research.* New York: Holt, Rinehart & Winston, Inc., 1965.

MEHRENS, W. A., and LEHMANN, I. J. *Standardized Tests in Education.* New York: Holt, Rinehart & Winston, Inc., 1969.

2

BASIC QUALITIES OF MEASURING INSTRUMENTS

In Chapter 1 we discussed a number of ways in which tests are and can be used in education. But, as with other products, there are good tests and bad tests; more precisely, tests attain the recommended standards for adequate measuring instruments in varying degrees. In this chapter we will describe the qualities that distinguish good tests, emphasizing those aspects that are most relevant to measurement in education. The reader should realize, however, that when evaluating tests for other purposes, different qualities may be more important.

STANDARDIZATION

A test, you will recall, was defined above as a systematic procedure for measuring the behavior of individuals. "Systematic" referred to three aspects of tests: their content, administration, and scoring. The process of attaining these systematic procedures is *standardization.*

The need for standard procedures should be obvious. Unless all individuals are presented with the same items under comparable testing conditions, and unless their scores are determined in the same manner, we will be comparing different types of performance. Thus the typical classroom recitation session and oral exams, while providing some information about students' knowledge, do not directly compare students, as each student answers a different set of questions. Only when students are administered the same items can their performance be compared.

Objectives

But even before we think about standardization, we must answer two questions: (1) What is the function of the testing? and (2) What outcomes or behaviors do we want to assess? As the former is usually "given"—that is, we know that we are, for example, testing to assign grades, to measure mastery of unit, or as a basis for sectioning students—we will concentrate on the latter question. These outcome behaviors are referred to as *objectives.*

Setting objectives is not as easy as it might seem on first blush. Consider, for example, an objective a third-grade teacher might set for an examination: "To measure students' understanding of currency." What does this objective really tell us? Nothing more than that the examination will deal with some aspects of the units in our monetary system. And what is meant by "understanding of currency"? We really don't know, except in a vague sense.

What is needed is a more precise definition of objectives. Particularly, most experts would ask that objectives be defined in behavioral terms, that we specify the behaviors which, when exhibited by the student, will indicate that he "knows" the material (Mager, 1962). Furthermore, we should specify the conditions under which he will display this knowledge and the level of proficiency expected. Applying these criteria to our example, the objective might be phrased:

> To test the student's understanding of currency by his ability to indicate (*a*) the correct amount of change and (*b*) the coins needed in transactions involving $10 or less, with 95 percent accuracy.

This alternative description specifies more precisely what behaviors students will be expected to exhibit.

Note that the objective has two dimensions: a content dimension and a behavioral (or skill) dimension. That is, we define both what content is covered (the currency system) and the behaviors to be exhibited (making change, or more basically, adding and subtracting amounts of money). Although standard lists of objectives have been developed (see, e.g., Bloom *et al.*, 1956), the teacher will probably want to define his own objectives to fit his particular instructional situation.

The importance of behavioral objectives is, of course, that unless we can unambiguously define what we are trying to measure we will never know if, in fact, we have succeeded in measuring what we intended to measure. Thus the first step is to define objectives.

Content

Given the objectives to be tapped by the test and the instructional materials used, we can specify the domain to be covered by the test. (Remember that we are talking about a content/skill domain.) But, since including enough items to cover all aspects of the domain is usually infeasible, a test will only sample the domain. Thus one important concern is the adequacy with which the test items sample the domain; this is the question of content validity (see below).

During standardization, the concern is with selecting a sample of items that can be administered to all students. One requirement of this sampling is, as was stated in the previous paragraph, that the items representatively sample the domain. Another requirement is to obtain items of proper difficulty. This level will vary depending on the group tested and purpose of the testing. For example, a test used to check if students have read an assignment would contain relatively easy items; a test used to select scholarship winners would include only very difficult items. Also, if several forms of the test are being developed, comparable samples of items must be obtained for every form.

In short, we try to select a sample of items of appropriate difficulty that representatively sample the domain being measured by the test.

Directions

Even if the same items are administered to all persons, scores will not be comparable unless everyone takes the test under similar conditions. To use an obvious example, if one student has 15 minutes to complete a long test and another receives an hour, the latter would have an advantage. Therefore, standard administrative procedures are needed to control the influence of extraneous variables. These procedures are usually communicated to the student through the test directions.

One major consideration is the length of the test in relation to the time needed to complete the test. A distinction can be made between speed tests and power tests. *Speed tests* contain simple items and are administered with a time limit set so that few, if any, persons can finish all items; the score is a measure of rate of response. A typing test would be a good example of a speed test. *Power tests*, in contrast, contain items of varying levels of difficulty, usually arranged (approximately) in order of difficulty, and time limits are set so that all[1] students can finish within the limits. Since, in education, we are primarily concerned with level of mastery, with the complexity of problems a student can solve, power tests are usually more appropriate than speed tests.

A related distinction is between tests of maximal performance and tests of typical performance (Cronbach, 1949). On a test of *maximal performance* a student is instructed to do his best, to attain his highest possible score; on a *typical performance* test the focus is on habitual performance. The set for typical or maximal performance is engendered by the test directions. Most educational tests, being achievement or ability tests, are measures of maximal performance. A concern, however, is that certain groups of students—often those from minority groups and/or disadvantaged backgrounds—will not regard the test as a situation demanding maximal performance; hence they may obtain spuriously low scores.

Another consideration is guessing. Should students be instructed to guess when unsure of the correct response? Although some authors are very concerned about the effects of guessing and suggest correcting test scores for guessing (Davis, 1964) the weight of the evidence (Ebel, 1965) would seem to indicate that correcting for guessing does not produce more accurate measurement. However, most test directions instruct students to guess when uncertain; this procedure, combined with no correction for guessing, rewards partial knowledge without penalizing unlucky guessers.

---

[1] For administrative convenience, time limits are generally set so that 90 percent or more of the students can attempt all items. These limits, coupled with the arrangement of items in order of difficulty, assure that almost all students will have time to obtain their maximum scores.

Scoring

The main goal is for scoring to be objective; objective in its broadest sense meaning agreement between competent scorers. Objective scoring procedures require three elements. First, there must be complete and immediate recording of responses. In most educational tests this requirement is met by students writing their answers, or indicating their choice among alternatives, on an answer sheet. Second, there must be a list of acceptable responses and variations of responses—a *scoring key*. On achievement and ability tests this is, of course, the list of correct answers. Third, a procedure must be specified for comparing each person's responses to the scoring key. This procedure may be as direct as using an electronic scoring machine or may involve judgment by the scorer, as when grading essay exams. In all cases the procedure must be detailed and unambiguous, so that trained scorers would agree on the scoring; otherwise, errors will be introduced by inconsistent scoring.

CONSISTENCY

A test score represents an individual's performance on a particular sample of items, administered at a particular time under a particular set of circumstances. Consequently it is only one estimate of a person's ability, not a precise and immutable index. Or, to use other words, every test score involves some measurement error. Even though standardization minimizes the effects of irrelevant variables, not all sources of error are eliminated. Thus a test score reflects both error-producing factors and "true" measurement of a trait, ability, or characteristic. The proportion of variability in test scores that is true (nonerror) is called the *consistency* or *reliability* of measurement.

What we are saying is that if an individual took the same test under different circumstances, or if he took a different test over the same material, he would not obtain exactly the same score. Examples from your own experience can illustrate. You have probably had the experience of taking a test on a day when you were ill, tired, or otherwise distracted and, consequently, did not perform up to par. Or, on a test requiring recording answers on a separate answer sheet, you may have mismarked some answers. Or you may have misunderstood the test directions and did not do what the tester expected you to do. The second point, that your score would be different on another sample of items, can also be easily illustrated. You may have had the experience of obtaining a high grade on a test because it just happened to stress material that you had studied intensively or obtained a low grade because the test stressed material that you had skimmed over. In each of these cases, you would have obtained a different score under different testing conditions. This is what is meant by measurement error.

One reason for desiring reliable measures is to minimize variability on retesting. Another reason is that we frequently relate test scores to other variables; if the scores themselves are not stable, we cannot find stable relations with other variables (which, themselves, may be less than completely invariant). If our tests measure consistently we have few problems; if not, problems may arise. Thus, as Kerlinger (1965) has pointed out, the reliability problem is like the money problem—it is only the lack of it that causes trouble.

Reliability Estimates

The study of reliability has proceeded on two separate but related levels—as a statistical theory of test scores (see, e.g., Ghiselli, 1964; Magnusson, 1966) and as a practical problem of test construction and use. We will discuss only the latter aspect.

Test users are primarily concerned with two types of consistency: consistency over time and consistency over forms of a test. In either case, reliability estimates are obtained by correlating scores on two administrations of a test to the same group. Correlation is a statistical technique for determining the degree of relationship (literally co-relation) between two sets of scores.[2] If scores on both tests fall in approximately the same order, the correlation coefficient will be high and positive (approaching a maximum value of 1.00 when there is a perfect relationship). If the two sets of scores are independent, they will correlate zero. If scores are related, but high scores on one test go with low scores on the other, the correlation will be negative. Thus, when estimating reliability, the higher the value of the correlation coefficient, the more consistent the scores and the less error of measurement.

One frequently used reliability estimate is the *coefficient of*

---

[2] Correlation and other descriptive statistics are briefly described in Appendix A.

stability or *test-retest reliability*. This index is derived by correlating scores on one administration of a test with scores on the same test administered at another time:

TEST———— (time) ————→ RETEST
⤹———————— correlation —————⤴

This coefficient, of course, measures how stable scores are over time. Anything that occurs during the interval between testings and differentially changes scores will reduce reliability. Thus this estimate is appropriate only when the characteristic being measured is presumed to be relatively stable and no important learning or maturation occurs between tests.

As a test represents only one possible sample of items, we might ask how the students would perform if given another form of the test (i.e., another sample of items). Estimates of consistency over test forms are called a *coefficient of equivalence* or *equivalent forms reliability*.

TEST: FORM A ———— (minimum time)————→TEST: FORM B
⤹———————— correlation —————⤴

Such estimates are, of course, meaningful only if the two test forms are, in fact, equivalent—i.e., contain parallel content, are equally difficult, and so on. As the tests are given nearly simultaneously, differences in performance are attributable to item sampling, rather than to changes in the individual.

It is, of course, possible to combine both methods and obtain a *coefficient of stability and equivalence:*

TEST: FORM A ———— (time) ————→TEST: FORM B
⤹———————— correlation ————⤴

This coefficient will produce the lowest estimate of reliability, as all factors that may influence performance—differences in individuals, test administration, and test content—have a chance to operate.

Internal Consistency

The perceptive reader will realize that the conditions described in the previous section seldom obtain in educational testing. For the most part, we do not administer the same test more than one time; when we do, we usually interpose some experience designed to change performance between the testings and thus render a stability estimate inappropriate. For example, one form of a test may be used as a pretest, an instructional unit presented, then a posttest administered to measure learning. Although the paradigm is comparable to that for test-retest reliability, the fact that the interposed experience was designed to change scores invalidates the method as an estimate of consistency.

How, then, can the teacher estimate the consistency of classroom and other *ad hoc* tests? Fortunately there are a number of methods available, all of which depend upon item interrelationships and are, accordingly, called internal consistency measures. The most widely used measures, the Kuder-Richardson formulae and Cronbach's coefficient alpha, involve computational procedures which render them infeasible unless automatic computation aids are available. Coefficient alpha, for example, is based on the average intercorrelation between test items. Internal consistency measures assume that all items on a test measure the same characteristics. Thus if a test is composed of items measuring widely divergent skills or abilities, an internal consistency estimate will be spuriously low and, hence, inappropriate.

Split-Half Reliability

A method that is frequently used with classroom test is *split-half reliability*. To compute this index a single form of a test is administered, the test items are divided into two pools (halves), and the correlation between halves is computed for a reliability estimate. If item positions were randomly assigned, this split can be between odd and even items; if the assignment was biased in some manner, more complex procedures will be needed to separate the halves. A split-half reliability estimate is, in many ways, similar to a coefficient of equivalence. However, it compares two tests, each of which is only half as long as the original test. As reliability is a function of test length—longer tests measure more consistently—the reliability as estimated from the halves of the test must be corrected by the Spearman-Brown formula. The corrected reliability estimate, which indicates how reliable a test of the original length would be, is the appropriate index of the test's reliability.

In our discussion we have mentioned that a test's reliability should be as high as possible. But what an acceptable level of reliability is depends on many variables—the type of test, what the scores will be used for, whether inferences will be made from individual scores, and so on. At an absolute level, reliability coefficients should be as close to 1.00 as possible; any lower value indicates the score contains some measurement error. On a more practical and comparative level, many standardized achievement and ability tests (the tests most often used in education) have reliabilities of .90–.95; thus tests with lower reliability should be looked upon with suspicion. The reliability of classroom tests is generally lower; reliabilities of .75–.80 are probably the minimum acceptable when individual scores are to be interpreted.

We should also stress that there is no one reliability for a test. A reliability coefficient indicates how consistently a test measures under a given set of circumstances; under a different set of circumstances the test's reliability will be different. This occurs because different sources of error are reflected in the various methods of estimating reliability. For example, a coefficient of stability measures consistency over time. Thus anything that occurs between the two testing sessions may influence the ordering of sources. In education, the most common effect is that students are exposed to different learning experiences; thus the amount of improvement (or forgetting) varies between students; consequently, reliability is lowered. Also, whenever two test administrations are involved, any factor which influences one administration but not the other (e.g., timing errors, distractions, students' physical and psychological condition) can reduce consistency. In contrast, methods involving only one test administration (e.g., split-half, internal consistency) eliminate differences due to test administration procedures as well as reduce differential learning and forgetting effects. In these situations, consistency will depend primarily on the comparability of the items comprising the test.

Two specific problems are worthy of note. As reliability is related to test length, subtest or part scores will generally be less reliable than total scores. And, as measurement errors tend to compound each other, the reliability of differences between pairs of scores will be much lower than the reliability of each individual score.

The measures of consistency discussed above all indicate how precisely a test measures. The teacher, however, often wants to know the answer to a slightly different question: How much would an individual's score vary if he were retested? For example, Suzy obtains an IQ of 103 on an individual intelligence test; we want to know if this score is an accurate index of her ability or if her score would be quite different on retesting. We can obtain an estimate of the expected variability (i.e., measurement error) from a statistic called the *standard error of measurement* (s_m).

The standard error of measurement is an index of the magnitude of measurement errors based on the variability of test scores and the test's reliability. It is possible to show that 68 percent of the time scores will vary by no more than $\pm 1\ s_m$ on retesting, and 95 percent of the time they will vary by no more than $\pm 2\ s_m$. Using our example, if we assume that s_m is 3 points, we can then say that there are approximately 2 chances out of 3 (68 percent) that Suzy's IQ will not vary by more than 3 points and only 1 chance in 20 that her score would change by more than 6 points. In other words, if Suzy were retested, there is only 1 chance in 20 that her score would fall outside the range 97–109.

VALIDITY

When studying consistency we were interested in the precision with which the test measured whatever it measured. We now turn to a more basic question: What does the test measure? This is the validity question.

Validity, like reliability and consistency, is a generic term which subsumes a variety of related concepts and procedures. Although over 40-odd types of validity can be identified, 3 major types predominate. These types ask the questions: How well does a test predict some behavior external to the test? What trait or characteristic underlies performance on the test? How well does the test represent the universe of situations of which the test items are but a sample? These types are called criterion-related validity, construct validity, and content validity, respectively.

Many uses of tests involve utilizing test scores to predict some behavior external to the test. For example, when using tests in selection we are predicting job performance or tenure. College admissions tests predict how students will probably perform academically in college. When test scores are used to assign students to different instructional methods, we are predicting which treatment will be optimal for each student. In each of these situations, test scores predict some extra-test behavior. This behavior is called the *criterion;* hence the term criterion-related validity. As the focus is on prediction, it is also called *predictive validity.*

The effectiveness of the test, its validity, is determined by how well scores predict the criterion behavior. Various methods can be used to determine predictive accuracy. The most widely used measure is the *validity coefficient,* which is the correlation between test scores and a criterion measure:

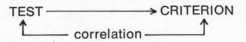

A validity coefficient shows the degree of relationship between test and criterion scores. The closer the relationship (the higher the validity coefficient) the more accurately the criterion can be predicted by test scores.

Another appropriate index is the number of correct decisions made using the test as a decision-making aid. Thus if we designate successful and unsuccessful ranges on the criterion and also set a cutting line of the test which discriminates between the accept (predict success) and reject (predict failure) regions, we have a fourfold table:

		Unsuccessful	Successful
Test scores	Accept	Miss	Hit
	Reject	Hit	Miss

Criterion

The upper right and lower left cells represent correct decisions (hits); the other two cells incorrect decisions (misses). The test's validity would be the proportion of correct decisions made (the hit rate).

These two methods of determining criterion-related validity can be illustrated by a study the author conducted at an engineering college. The question was how well a particular math test could predict students' grade averages during the freshman year. As one approach, we correlated test scores and grade averages. The correlation (validity coefficient) was .47, indicating that math test scores were, in fact, related to grade averages; that is, students who obtained higher test scores also obtained higher grades. We also looked at how many correct decisions would be made using the test:

Test score	Grade Average	
	Below C	C or above
41 or above	124	470
40 or below	57	32

That is, using a minimum cutting score of 41, we would correctly classify 527 out of the 683 students—the 470 who were predicted to obtain at least a C average and did so and the 57 who were predicted to obtain below a C average and did so—and incorrectly classify the other 156 students. In other words, we would make correct predictions for 77 percent of the students.

In education, criterion-related validity is relevant whenever we predict future performance. Thus it is particularly useful when evaluating aptitude tests and procedures used in selection and placement of students. It is of less value when evaluating achievement tests, such as classroom examinations.

Construct Validity

Construct validity attempts to answer the question: What psychological trait underlies the test? As such, it is most relevant in personality measurement and for tests designed to measure "basic" human abilities and traits; it is of limited concern to most classroom teachers. The procedure in construct validation is roughly analogous to the general scientific method. Given a theory which includes the trait which the test measures, we can hypothesize how test scores, if they do measure the trait, will relate to other measures or vary under different (experimental) conditions. We can then subject the hypothesis to empirical test; the results will strengthen or weaken our acceptance of the theory. Repetitions of this procedure will gradually sharpen the definition of the trait and thereby clarify the meaning of the test scores. (For a basic treatment of construct validity, see Cronbach and Meehl, 1955.)

Content Validity

The type of validity that is most relevant to the educational setting is content validity. Its importance rests on the fact that it is the primary method used to evaluate achievement tests, and achievement tests are the most frequently used tests in education.

The basic question in content validity is: Are the test items a representative sample of the domain (universe) being measured by the test? We have previously noted that, when developing a test, we must first define objectives, the content and skills (behaviors) to be measured by the test. We then select items to representatively sample this domain. The more adequately the items reflect the underlying domain, the more confidently we can generalize from test performance and make statements about the person's performance in the universe of situations being sampled by the test. Thus if a test measuring skill in performing arithmetic operations contained addition, subtraction, multiplication, *and* division problems of varying complexity, we would feel safe in generalizing from an individual's test score to make statements about his ability to perform basic arithmetic operations. If, however, the test consisted of only simple addition problems, we would not feel justified in generalizing much beyond the test scores; certainly not to make statements about his arithmetic ability.

You can note that, in contrast to criterion-related validity, there is no completely objective way of determining content validity nor a single quantitative index of the degree of content validity. Rather, content validity is based on the judgment of the test reviewer. It should also be noted that an accurate judgment of content validity cannot be made unless the domain being sampled has been precisely defined—again the need for behavioral objectives shows through. This last statement, however, should not be taken to mean that the reviewer must accept the objectives as defined by the test developer. He may make his own specification of the domain and then judge how well the test samples the domain as he has now defined it. For example, when using a standardized achievement test in a given school, the test will be useful (valid) to the extent that it assesses the objectives of that particular school, not to the extent that the test developer has met the objectives as he defined them.[3] In other words, validity, be it content or criterion-related, is situation specific.

One other type of validity, *face validity*, is frequently confused with content validity. A test has face validity when the test items appear to measure what the test is supposed to measure. Although, superficially, face validity and content validity may appear similar, they are quite different. Content validity is determined by a thorough review of the test by the test user; face validity is based on a casual perusal by the test taker. The importance of face validity is motivational—unless the test appears to be a fair measure to the test taker, his motivation when taking the test may be inappropriate.

Finally it should be noted that all types of validity may apply to the same test. To illustrate, a vocabulary test might demonstrate criterion-related validity by predicting grades in English courses, construct validity as a measure of verbal intelligence, and content validity as an exam for a course in vocabulary building. Or a final examination in a math course (content validity) may also be used as an index of numerical reasoning (construct validity) and to predict grades in science courses (criterion-related validity).

PRACTICAL CONSIDERATIONS

Many of the practical considerations in testing have been alluded to, directly or inferentially, in the previous discussion as they may influence reliability or validity or are controlled through standardization. Thus we will but mention some of the more important ones. The editorial quality—the writing style, layout, and printing—of the test should be of good quality. The time limits should not place undue emphasis on speed nor be so long as to introduce boredom or fatigue; hopefully they will be compatible with the length of class periods. Answer sheets and other response

---

[3] This task is made easier if the test developer indicates what each test item presumably measures. For example, the manual for the Iowa Tests of Basic Skills indicates the specific skill which each item is designed to measure (e.g., use of comma to separate words in a series, ability to locate places on a map through use of a key). To determine the content validity of the ITBS for his class, the teacher would compare the distribution of skills measured by the test items to his estimate of the importance of the various skills. If the correspondence were high, the test would possess content validity for this situation.

procedures should be clear and simple. Administrative procedures should not be unduly complex and should be appropriate to the age and sophistication of test takers.

On standardized tests, manuals explaining the administration, scoring, and interpretation of scores should be available, as should technical data on the construction, standardization, reliability, and validity of the test. Equivalent test forms are often desirable for retesting and other purposes. The test user should also investigate what auxiliary services, such as machine scoring, the publisher may provide.

Most practical considerations are closely tied to the costs of testing. Ideally, the cost of any testing program should be minimal consistent with attaining the desired quality. Costs may be (1) both immediate and direct—e.g., the costs of test booklets, answer sheets, scoring; (2) direct but spread over several years—e.g., separate answer sheets and reusable booklets will reduce long-term costs; or (3) indirect—e.g., the time and personnel needed to make the administrative arrangements and interpret scores to teachers, students, and parents.

One way of evaluating the costs of a test is to consider its *utility*. Determination of utility is a complex procedure, but basically it combines validity and financial considerations in a costs/benefits analysis. That is, the benefits accrued from correct decisions made using the test (say, students accepted into an educational program who succeed) are plus factors; the losses from incorrect decisions (accepting a student who drops out, rejecting a potentially successful applicant) and the cost of the selection program are negatives; the algebraic sum is the utility of the program. Thus a test may be valid yet result in a net loss because of its high cost. Such analyses are most appropriate when definite values can be assigned to various outcomes, a situation that usually does not obtain in education.

SUMMARY

In this chapter we have considered some important qualities that must be considered when developing, selecting, evaluating, or interpreting a test. We started with the process of standardization —the development of procedures for assuring that the testing process is comparable for all students. We then considered consistency of measurement and the methods for estimating how consistently (reliably) a test measured—over time, test forms, and/or items. The third consideration was validity—how well the test measures the characteristic it measures or does the job it was designed to do. The concept of content validity, which is central to educational measurement, was stressed. Finally, we briefly mentioned some practical considerations.

One very important consideration—normative data for interpreting scores—was not discussed but will be the subject of the following chapter.

REFERENCES

BLOOM, B. S., *et al. Taxonomy of Educational Objectives.* (Handbook I, *Cognitive Domain.*) New York: David McKay Co., Inc., 1956.

CRONBACH, L. J. *Essentials of Psychological Testing.* New York: Harper & Row, Publishers, 1949.

CRONBACH, L. J., and MEEHL, P. E. "Construct Validity in Psychological Tests," *Psychological Bulletin,* Vol. 52 (1955), pp. 281–302.

DAVIS, F. B. *Educational Measurements and Their Interpretation.* Belmont, Calif.: Wadsworth Publishing Co., Inc., 1964.

EBEL, R. L. *Measuring Educational Achievement.* Englewood Cliffs, N.J.: Prentice-Hall, Inc., 1965.

GHISELLI, E. E. *Theory of Psychological Measurement.* New York: McGraw-Hill Book Co., 1964.

KERLINGER, F. N. *Foundations of Behavioral Research.* New York: Holt, Rinehart & Winston, Inc., 1965.

MAGER, R. F. *Preparing Objectives for Programmed Instruction.* San Francisco: Fearon Publishers, Inc., 1962.

MAGNUSSON, D. *Test Theory.* Reading, Mass.: Addison-Wesley Publishing Co., Inc., 1966.

3

TEST SCORES AND THEIR INTERPRETATION

To interpret test scores we must have two types of information. First, we need to know what the test measures and/or what criteria its scores predict; that is, we need validity data. Second, we need a standard or scale for describing performance. Ideally, intrinsically meaningful scales that describe performance in "absolute" terms—scales comparable to those for measuring distance or weight—would be available. Unfortunately, such scales are not as prevalent in educational and psychological measurement as in physical measurement; in fact, examples are almost impossible to find. Thus, in educational measurement, an individual's score usually is interpreted by comparing it to the performance of other individuals who are, in some relevant ways, similar to him. Such measurement is interindividual or *normative*.

NORMATIVE DATA

In order to interpret scores, therefore, we must know how a group of persons performed on the test; then any individual's score can be compared to this group, the *norm group*. An individual score can, potentially, be compared to many different groups; which particular groups will be appropriate will depend on the characteristics members of the norm groups share with the test taker. For example, to interpret the performance of Mabel Morris on a standardized biology test we might compare her scores to a norm group composed of students who are in the same grade, who attend the same type of school, who live in the same section of the country, and who are enrolled in a biology course.

Which particular dimensions or characteristics distinguish the relevant norm groups will, as indicated previously, depend upon the purposes of the testing. Dimensions which frequently are relevant in educational testing include: sex, age, grade, type of school, type of community, geographical area, and type of course or curriculum. In some circumstances test-defined characteristics may be used; for example, on achievement tests separate norms might be developed for students of average, above average, and below average intelligence. As indicated in the example in the previous paragraph, norm groups generally will be defined by several, not just one, dimension.

As comparisons with different norm groups will provide different information, several norm groups may be used. For example, a student's scores on an end-of-year achievement battery may be compared to (1) his classmates, (2) other students in the same grade in the school system, and (3) a national or regional sample of children in the same grade. These various comparisons will provide complementary information.

Regardless of the particular norm group used, certain questions can be asked to evaluate the adequacy of the normative data. First, are the dimensions of the population clearly specified? To know only that a norm group is composed of college freshmen tells us little; we need to know what types of colleges were sampled, on what basis students were selected, and what characteristics distinguish students in the norm group. In short, we need to know precisely what sort of persons comprise the norm group. Second, does the norm group representatively sample the population? Generally, a norm group will be a sample rather than an entire population; therefore, nonrepresentative sampling will produce misleading data. As it is often easier to collect certain types of data (for example, it is easier to obtain test scores from relatively wealthy suburban schools than from central-city ghetto schools), possible sampling biases must be considered. Third, is the sample large enough so the data will be stable and reliable? No minimum sample size can be specified;[1] however, a small, well-defined sam-

---

[1] As stability will be proportional to sample size, larger samples are preferable. A minimum of several hundred cases is usually necessary for acceptable stability; beyond this level, the gain in stability must be balanced against the added costs of obtaining larger samples of scores.

ple is preferable to a larger, poorly specified one. Fourth, were the scores collected recently enough to be still appropriate? With admissions requirements, instructional methods, and curricula changing continuously, normative data may rapidly become out-dated.

Fifth, and most important, are the available normative data relevant to your purposes? Again, the user will have to define what is relevant. Generally, in education, the minimal requirement will be that the norm group be composed of students of the same educational level who have experienced the same type of curricula as the person whose scores are to be interpreted. (That is, we compare students taking "new math" to other students who have taken "new math," not to students taught traditional math.) Beyond this, the user will have to define the relevant dimensions for himself.

Local Norms

With standardized tests, the test publisher will generally provide several sets of normative data. These data will necessarily be based on broadly defined groups. Thus if the test user wants to use norms based on his own school system, he will have to develop local norms. Local norms are nothing more than norms derived from a sample of students from the local setting. Development of local norms is quite straightforward (see Chapter 5) and can be done by local personnel. In addition, some test publishers provide scoring and norming services. The advantage of local norms is, of course, that they can be used to compare students to their immediate peers and/or competitors.

TYPES OF SCORES

When we score a test or examination we usually record the number of items answered correctly, the number of errors, the total number of points credit, or some similar score. Such a score, obtained directly from the test, is called a *raw score*. Raw scores, by themselves, have little, if any, meaning. What, for example, does a score of 18 on a spelling test mean? Even knowing that the test contained 25 items is of little help; we want to know if 18 was the highest score in the class, an above average score, in the middle range, below average, or the lowest score in the class. Until the raw score is compared to a norm group, its meaning is unclear.

To aid interpretation, raw scores are often converted to another scale. Perhaps the most common conversion in education is to a *percentage scale*—18 out of 25 correct is 72 percent. But percentage scores have the same defects as raw scores. Moreover, they imply that an absolute level of performance has been established, an implication that generally is not true.

A number of other converted (derived or transformed) scores are in common use; in the following section we will describe the most common ones. Our approach will be to describe each score and its interpretation but say little about its computation. The reader interested in the derivations and computations of these scores should see Brown (1970, Chapter 7) or Lyman (1963).

Percentiles

One widely used derived score system is percentiles. A *percentile rank* can be defined as a [person's] relative rank in a norm group expressed in percentage terms. Thus, a percentile rank of 78 indicates that the person scored higher than 78 percent of the norm group and lower than the other 22 percent. Similarly, a percentile rank of 13 represents a score higher than 13 percent of the scores and lower than 87 percent of the scores. Note that percentile ranks refer to percentage of scores (or people), not percentage of items answered correctly. Note also that percentiles are an ordinal scale; they denote rankings but tell nothing about differences between scores.

One can also find the raw score equivalent of any percentile rank. This point, called a *percentile point*, is useful when dividing a group into sections. For example, the 75th percentile point will separate the top quarter from the remainder of a group.

The main advantages of percentiles are their ease of computation[2] and comprehension (the only possible problem is confusing them with percentage scores). Their major disadvantages are that they indicate only ranking and thus may present problems for statistical analyses, and that small raw score differences near the center of a score distribution are associated with relatively large percentile differences (see Figure 3.1). Thus differences between percentile ranks may be overinterpreted, particularly in the average score range.

---

[2] See Chapter 5.

If statistical analyses of test scores are to be made, a scale having equal-sized units (i.e., an interval scale) is preferable. The problem is to find a scale whose units (1) are of the same size throughout the score range and (2) are psychologically meaningful. In educational and psychological testing the usual practice is to express individual scores in terms of their deviation from the average score of a reference (norm) group.

To compute standard scores, therefore, we must both know the average score (the *mean*, symbolized $\overline{X}$) and have a measure of variability. The measure of variability used is the standard deviation[3] (symbolized s). Then any individual score (called X) can be expressed as a deviation from the mean ($X - \overline{X}$ or x) in standard deviation units:

$$z = \frac{X - \overline{X}}{s} = \frac{x}{s} \tag{3.1}$$

The z score is called a *standard score* because it expresses performance in standard deviation units.

To explain why this particular procedure produces an interval scale is beyond the scope of this book; the reader will have to accept it on faith or refer to a book on the theory of psychological measurement (e.g., Guilford, 1954; Ghiselli, 1964).

The advantage of standard scores is that they have constant meaning from one score distribution to another; thus scores on two tests can be compared if both are expressed as standard scores. That is, a standard score of $+1$ ($z = 1.0$) indicates a score 1 standard deviation above the mean, regardless of the distribution used. Furthermore, by using the normal curve as a model, standard scores can be translated into percentile ranks (see Figure 3.1). Thus a standard score of $+1$ is equivalent to a percentile rank of 84.

Because z scores involve decimals and negative numbers, they are usually transformed to yet another scale, making use of the mathematical principle that, on an interval scale, one can multiply by a constant or add a constant to each score without destroying the relationship between pairs of scores. Although any set of constants can be used (and different ones are used on various tests)

---

[3] See Appendix A.

FIGURE 3.1   THE RELATIONSHIP BETWEEN RAW SCORES, PERCENTILES. AND STANDARD SCORES

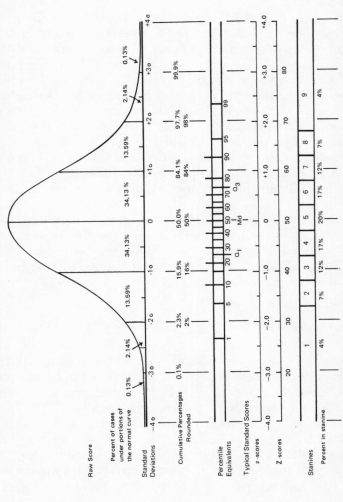

Note: This chart shows the relationships when the raw score distribution is normal. Distributions of actual test data will not, of course, be distributed normally, and thus the relationship will only approximate those shown.

Source: Adapted from H. G. Seashore, *Methods of Expressing Test Scores* (Test Service Bulletin No. 48 [New York: The Psychological Corporation, 1955]).

the recommended procedure (APA, 1966) is to transform scores to a scale having a mean of 50 and a standard deviation of 10 units:

$$Z = 50 + 10z \tag{3.2}$$

and rounding to whole numbers. This new scale retains the original relationships between scores but eliminates the undesirable features of z scores.

Standard scores (z and Z), as described above, follow the peculiarities of the raw score distribution. For many purposes (e.g., in developing normative data for standardized tests), a normal distribution of scores would be preferable. It is possible to force raw scores into standard scores having a normal distribution by utilizing the areas of the normal curve as the basis of transformation. Scores derived in this manner, called *normalized standard scores,* are used on most standardized tests. If the original raw score distribution is approximately normal, the transformation serves only to smooth or correct the distribution and thus is appropriate; if the original distribution departs widely from normality, the transformation will, of course, distort the distribution and be inappropriate.

Another variety is *stanines.* The stanine scale is a nine step (standard nine) scale, whose middle seven steps are .5s wide (see Figure 3.1). Its advantages are the convenience of its one-digit score and the lessened risk of overinterpreting small differences by using a smaller range of scores.

Developmental Scales

When measuring a characteristic which varies in some systematic way with developmental level, an individual can be assigned as a score the developmental level which his performance typifies. The most common examples are age and grade scales.

To build an *age scale* we first have to determine the average performance of children of various ages. Next we draw a curve showing the relationship between scores and age (see Figure 3.2). Then whenever a student takes the test, he would be assigned as a score the age that his performance typifies. In our example, a student scoring 35 would be assigned an age score of 7–6. This score means that his performance was comparable to the average child 7 years and 6 months old.

FIGURE 3.2
A HYPOTHETICAL GROWTH CURVE

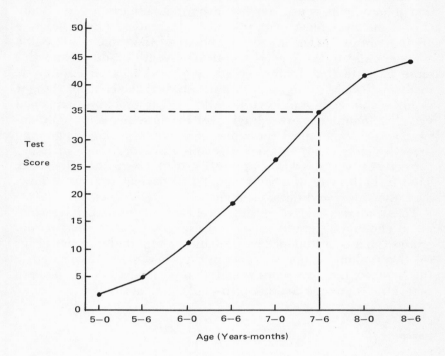

Note: To find the age score equivalent of a test score, draw a perpendicular from the test score to the curve, then another at right angles from the curve to the horizontal axis; the point of intersection with the horizontal axis will be the age score assigned.

Grade scales are developed and interpreted in an analogous manner, only, of course, using grade level rather than age as the point of reference. Both age and grade scores are easy to understand and make good sense as long as the characteristic changes systematically and regularly with age (or grade). However, when the growth rate slows or fluctuates, interpretation problems may arise. For example, when mental growth slows in adult years one year may produce but little change in performance; thus age scores would be misleading. Grade scales bear the further assumption that the same materials are always taught at a particular grade level.

There is a common misinterpretation of grade scores. Suppose that Johnny, who is just starting fifth grade, obtains a grade score of 7–2 on an achievement test in mathematics. (Remember, a grade score of 7–2 means that he obtained the same score as the average child in the second month of seventh grade.) Does this score indicate that Johnny could be placed in a seventh-grade mathematics class? No, as he has not studied the concepts taught in fifth- and sixth-grade mathematics. What probably happened was that Johnny did exceedingly well on those items he could answer and thus obtained the same score as the average beginning seventh grader who, although answering a wider range of items, correctly answered a lower proportion of the items he attempted. That is, both made the same number of correct responses; however, they answered different items.

To avoid this sort of misinterpretation, many experts recommend eliminating grade scores and using *percentile ranks within grades*. That is, a student's performance is reported in terms of his relative ranking among students in the same grade. Expressed in this manner, Johnny's score would be reported as, say, at the 98th percentile compared to other fifth-grade students.

Ratios

Perhaps the most famous test score is the *intelligence quotient,* or *IQ.* The IQ as originally developed was the ratio between a child's mental age (an age score as defined above) and his chronological age, multiplied by 100; that is:

$$IQ = \frac{\text{mental age (M.A.)}}{\text{chronological age (C.A.)}} \times 100$$

This score was a *ratio IQ.* Analyses of normative data showed that the rate of mental growth slowed down in the teens and twenties and corrections had to be applied when computing the ratio IQ. Thus many individual intelligence tests now use a form of normalized standard scores as IQ's; these scores are properly called *deviation IQ's.*

The illustration points out one problem with ratio scores—they are properly computed only using ratio scales (scales having a true zero point and equal-sized units), and most psychological tests do not yield ratio scores. Another problem is that the ratio of two unreliable scores compounds the errors in the individual scores. In addition, so-called achievement quotients (achievement test scores/intelligence test scores) and related ratios often make assumptions that may not be psychologically tenable, that is, that students should achieve at a level commensurate with their measured intelligence and/or that intelligence is the only factor determining achievement. Thus ratio scores should generally be taken with a grain of salt.

PRESENTING NORMATIVE DATA

Having discussed norm groups and described some common types of scores, we now will consider how normative information is summarized and communicated.

Conversion Tables

Most test manuals present normative data in conversion tables (norm tables). These are nothing more than charts showing derived score equivalents of raw scores. A conversion table may utilize several types of derived scores or only one. More complex tables show the performance of several tests or subtests. (Note that these latter tables permit comparisons of the relative performance of different groups and the relative difficulty of several tests, respectively, as well as providing a basis for interpreting individual scores.) As performance will be interpreted relative to a specific group, a description of the norm group should always be included with the table.

An illustration of a conversion table is given in Figure 3.3. This table shows the raw score equivalents of various percentile points on the tests in the Differential Aptitude Test battery for a norm group composed of eighth-grade males.[4] Scores are interpreted by reading across rows. For example, on the Verbal Reasoning test a raw score of 30 is associated with a percentile rank of 85; the same raw score on the Mechanical Reasoning test would produce a percentile rank of 10.

---

[4] A more complete description of the norm group can be found in the test manual.

FIGURE 3.3
AN ILLUSTRATIVE CONVERSION TABLE
FALL (First Semester) PERCENTILE NORMS

FORM L
GRADE 8F

N = 2200+

Raw Scores

BOYS Percentile	Verb. Reas.	Num. Abil.	VR + NA	Abst. Reas.	Clerical S and A	Mech. Reas.	Space Rela.	LU-I: Spell.	LU-II: Gram.	Percentile
99	41–50	34–40	69–90	43–50	70–100	60–68	51–60	89–100	45–60	99
97	38–40	32–33	63–68	42	64–69	58–59	47–50	85–88	41–44	97
95	34–37	29–31	58–62	41	58–63	55–57	43–46	80–84	36–40	95
90	31–33	27–28	54–57	39–40	55–57	53–54	39–42	75–79	33–35	90
85	28–30	26	51–53	37–38	53–54	51–52	35–38	71–74	31–32	85
80	26–27	24–25	48–50	36	51–52	49–50	32–34	66–70	29–30	80
75	24–25	22–23	45–47	35	50	48	30–31	65–67	27–28	75
70	22–23	21	42–44	33–34	48–49	47	28–29	62–64	25–26	70
65	21	20	40–41	32	46–47	46	26–27	60–61	24	65
60	19–20	19	38–39	31	45	45	24–25	58–59	23	60
55	18	18	36–37	30	44	44	23	56–57	22	55
50	17	17	34–35	28–29	43	42–43	22	54–55	21	50
45	16	16	32–33	27	42	41	21	52–53	20	45
40	15	15	30–31	26	41	40	20	51	18–19	40
35	14	14	29	24–25	39–40	39	19	49–50	17	35
30	13	13	27–28	22–23	37–38	37–38	17–18	48	16	30
25	12	12	25–26	19–21	35–36	35–36	15–16	46–47	15	25
20	11	11	23–24	16–18	34	33–34	13–14	44–45	13–14	20
15	9–10	10	21–22	13–15	32–33	31–32	12	41–43	11–12	15
10	8	9	19–20	10–12	28–31	29–30	11	38–40	9–10	10
5	7	7–8	16–18	7–9	23–27	26–28	10	32–37	7–8	5
3	6	5–6	13–15	4–6	15–22	22–25	9	25–31	6	3
1	0–5	0–4	0–12	0–3	0–14	0–21	0–8	0–24	0–5	1
Mean	18.8	17.8	36.6	27.1	42.9	42.2	24.4	56.3	22.2	Mean
SD	8.7	6.9	14.2	10.4	11.0	9.0	10.3	14.6	8.7	SD

Source: Adapted from G. K. Bennett, H. G. Seashore, and A. G. Wesman, *Manual for the Differential Aptitude Tests* (4th ed.; New York: The Psychological Corporation, 1966), p. 3–8. Reproduced by permission. Copyright 1947, 1952 © 1959, 1963, 1966 by The Psychological Corporation, New York, N.Y. All rights reserved.

When several scores are to be interpreted simultaneously, a visual profile is often an effective presentation method. A profile consists of scores on several tests plotted on the same graph. Viewing a profile, one can readily identify high scores, low scores, the relationship of various scores to each other, the scatter of scores, and other relevant information.

A profile can be plotted in any score units—percentiles, standard scores, age scores—or even general categories, e.g., high, above average, below average, and low. The governing considerations will be the degree of precision needed and meaningfulness to persons viewing the profile. One particularly useful type is the *normal percentile chart*. This chart uses percentiles as units but scales them on a standard score scale to prevent overinterpretation of small percentile differences in the average score range. An example is shown in Figure 3.4. One caution is needed when constructing and interpreting profiles. Unless all scores are derived from the same norm group, they will not be directly comparable, as they will compare the performance of diverse groups of students.

Expectancy Tables

The methods discussed previously showed only an individual's ranking within a norm group; validity was not considered. However, if we had evidence of the test's validity in a particular (normative) group, we could infer that persons obtaining higher test scores would also obtain higher criterion scores. Thus it would be preferable to combine validity and normative data more directly. One method is by using expectancy tables.

An *expectancy table* shows the expected outcome associated with a given test score. Thus it combines validity and normative data and interprets performance, not as a ranking within a group, but in outcome terms. Construction of an expectancy table is simple (see, e.g., Wesman, 1949), requiring only that the relative frequencies of various possible outcomes be determined for each score range. The same data could, of course, be presented in other ways, e.g., graphically. The important point, however, is that scores can be interpreted in outcome terms.

An example of a simple expectancy table is presented in Figure 3.5. More complex tables, utilizing several predictor variables, could have been illustrated. This particular expectancy table

FIGURE 3.4

AN EXAMPLE OF A NORMAL PERCENTILE CHART

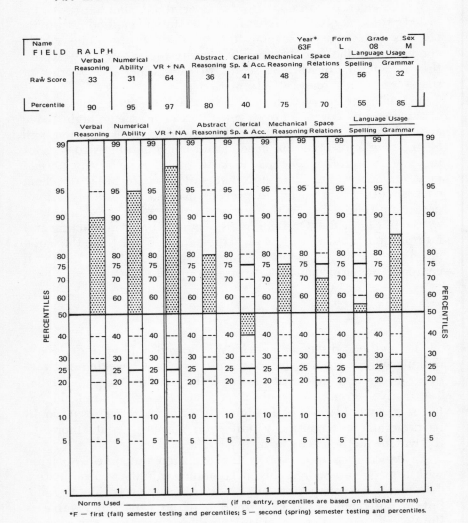

Source: Adapted from the G. K. Bennett, H. G. Seashore, and A. G. Wesman, *Manual for the Differential Aptitude Tests* (4th ed.; New York: The Psychological Corporation, 1966), p. 3–6. Reproduced by permission. Copyright 1947, 1952 © 1959, 1963, 1966 by The Psychological Corporation, New York, N.Y. All rights reserved.

FIGURE 3.5

AN EXAMPLE OF AN EXPECTANCY TABLE

Expectancy table showing the probability of attaining a C average or above during the freshman year; College of Engineering, Midwest State University (*N* = 799; Probability expressed as chances in 100).

High School Rank	C Average	Probability Below C
Top 10%	92	8
Second 10%	69	31
Third 10%	61	39
Fourth 10%	49	51
Fifth 10%	43	57
Sixth 10%	36	64
Lower 40%	29	71

shows the probability of attaining a C average in an engineering college, dependent upon the student's rank in his high school graduating class. As can be seen, the probabilities range from 92 percent, for students who were in the top tenth of their high school class, to 29 percent, for students who graduated in the lower 40 percent of their class.

CONTENT SCORES

The scores that we have discussed are normative and compare an individual's performance to that of other people. Although knowing Johnny's relative ranking provides useful information, in many circumstances we would prefer scores which would tell us what Johnny can do, what skills he has mastered, or how he can or will perform—scores that are interpretable in criterion terms, that compare an individual to a standard rather than to other people. Glaser (1963) has labeled these scores *criterion-referenced*, in contrast to the more traditional approach, which he calls *norm-referenced*. The two types are complementary, not antagonistic.

Of the scores we have discussed, expectancy tables and developmental scales probably come closest to being criterion-referenced. Expectancy tables report performance in outcome (criterion) terms; however, the criterion scale used generally reflects a practically useful dimension, rather than a systematic attempt to define transsituational performance levels. Age and grade scales may have an element of criterion-referencing, yet because they scale scores to the average performance of a group, basically they are normative in nature.

A number of attempts to develop criterion-referenced (content) scores have been made, but without a notable degree of success. The main stumbling block is not the construction of tests to measure skill levels but rather defining the various levels of performance. It is one thing to say that a scale measuring various levels of reading ability is needed; it is a much more difficult task to define these levels. Progress has been made in areas such as mathematics, where skills cumulate and criterion performance can be precisely specified—e.g., the ability to multiply pairs of three-digit numbers with less than 10 percent errors (see Glaser, 1968).

Ebel (1962) has pointed out that there are two methods for developing content scales. One is to thoroughly and precisely specify the domain and the item construction process, standardize testing conditions, and use the percent of maximal possible performance as a score (cf. the example in the previous paragraph). This procedure is appropriate only when the domain can be precisely defined and proceeds from the domain to the test score. An alternative procedure goes in the other direction, from test scores to performance standards. In this approach, the skills and abilities of persons attaining each score level would be ascertained. Knowing an individual's test score, we could then specify the characteristics that typify the behavior of persons attaining this score. This approach is feasible even when a domain cannot be precisely delimited.

The implications of criterion-referenced measurement are several. Most important, we could describe ability in terms more directly relevant to the educational process. Second, test construction procedures would be changed. Objectives would play a greater role in item selection, and statistical concepts based on differences between individuals would be inappropriate in their present form (Popham and Husek, 1969). Third, there could be even closer ties between testing and the evaluation of instruction (see Chapter 9). And, of course, traditional types of normative data would be inappropriate.

FACTORS IN TEST INTERPRETATION

The process of interpreting test scores is complicated by several considerations beyond what scoring system and normative group are to be used. First, as we have repeatedly mentioned, the interpreter must constantly keep in mind what the test measures. When scores are expressed in criterion terms, as in expectancy tables and content scores, this problem is minimal. When a test is used as a predictor, but scores are not expressed in criterion terms, one must be aware of what outcomes the test has demonstrated its ability to predict—its criterion-related validity. When content validity is central, the interpreter must have a clear idea of the domain being sampled by the test. For example, a "French test" might measure comprehension of spoken French, understanding of the written language, knowledge of French vocabulary, ability to translate English into French, ability to speak French, knowledge of French grammar, familiarity with the French culture, or some combination of these skills. An appreciation of the content and skills measured by the test can be gained only by thorough study of the test items.

Second, besides the validity question, we must also consider reliability data. No test measures without error. Thus every test score is an approximation to the individual's "true" score; the more reliable the test, the closer the approximation. Because of the presence of measurement errors, many people recommend that test scores be interpreted, not as precise points, but as ranges or *bands*. Some test publishers even build score bands into their scoring and/or profiling procedures. Thus, instead of saying that Mary scored at the 75th percentile, we might say that Mary's score placed her between the 70th and 80th percentiles. The width of the band used is based on some measure of variability, such as the standard error of measurement.

As measurement errors tend to compound themselves, differences between pairs of scores will be more unstable than either individual score. The test user may encounter this problem in several places: when considering differences between subtests or tests in a test battery (e.g., between the arithmetic concepts and arithmetic operations sections of an achievement battery); when comparing scores from different tests (e.g., comparing achievement and ability test scores); and when considering gains (from a pretest to a posttest) during an instructional sequence or from year to year. In each case, the tendency is to interpret small chance differences as if they indicated a true difference or change.

Third, one frequently hears the recommendation that a score on one test be substituted for a score on another, presumably equivalent, test. For example, a student may have taken one college admissions test, say the ACT, only to find that one school he is applying to requires another test, the College Board's SAT. The question is raised: Why can't the ACT scores be substituted for SAT scores, as both are college admissions tests? Although there are methods of obtaining comparable scores on two tests—comparable meaning equivalent rankings in the same group—these procedures do not produce equivalent scores. To be truly equivalent, scores must not only be comparable, but the content of the two tests must be highly similar (Wesman, 1958). This requirement generally is not met. And, because some content is unique to each test, the tests are not necessarily measuring the same abilities, even if they have similar names. Furthermore, their unique aspects may make one or the other more appropriate and/or valid in any particular setting.

Fourth, although a test score tells us *how well* the individual performed in the testing situation, rarely does it tell *why* he performed as he did. A test score is a product of an individual's inherited characteristics, his learning and experiences to the time of the testing, and the testing situation. All of these factors must be considered when interpreting scores. To give but two obvious examples: A student who was not motivated for maximal performance when taking an ability test will probably attain a score that underestimates his ability; a student who takes an achievement test in a subject matter area which stresses concepts and methods other than those stressed in his courses will also obtain a lower score than he would on a test whose emphases were more compatible with his experiences. Thus many factors have to be taken into account when interpreting scores. The danger, however, is that we will try to explain away a person's test performance (particularly if his performance was poor or lower than expected) and forget that many of the same factors that influenced his test performance may also affect his performance in other situations.

Finally, when interpreting test scores to other persons—students, parents, other school personnel—we must consider how the score will be interpreted by the person receiving the information and how this will affect him. For example, what will be the effect of telling a student that his intelligence test scores indicate that he can do much better work? Of telling a college professor that his son has below average academic ability? Or, of telling a student that he obtained the highest possible score on a very difficult test? Thus to interpret scores effectively one must be conversant with the technicalities of measurement as well as have skills in communicating information to others. (See Goldman, 1961, for an excellent discussion of test use and interpretation.)

SUMMARY

Learning how to interpret tests can only be accomplished by working with actual test scores. In this chapter we have tried to provide some of the necessary technical groundwork by presenting the principles underlying test scores. We first discussed the function of norm groups, then considered various common types of scores. Our approach was descriptive, attempting to provide an understanding of the various types of scores and normative data rather than to develop skill in deriving the scores. Finally, we discussed some problems and considerations in interpreting scores.

Several themes recur throughout the chapter: the fact that test interpretation must be based on both validity and normative data; the need for precisely defining the norm group the person is being compared with and understanding the limitations of the scores used; the relativistic nature of most psychological and educational measurement; and the differences between norm-referenced and criterion-referenced measurement.

REFERENCES

AMERICAN PSYCHOLOGICAL ASSOCIATION. *Standards for Educational and Psychological Tests and Manuals.* Washington, D.C., 1966.

BROWN, F. G. *Principles of Educational and Psychological Testing.* Hinsdale, Ill.: The Dryden Press, 1970.

EBEL, R. L. "Content Standard Test Scores," *Educational and Psychological Measurement,* Vol. 22, (1962), pp. 15–25.

GHISELLI, E. E. *Theory of Psychological Measurement.* New York: McGraw-Hill Book Co., 1964.

GLASER, R. "Instructional Technology and the Measurement of Learning Outcomes: Some Questions," *American Psychologist,* Vol. 18 (1963), pp. 519–21.

GLASER, R. "Adapting the Elementary School Curriculum to Individual Performance," in *Proceedings of the 1967 Invitational Conference on Testing Problems,* pp. 3–36. Princeton, N.J.: Educational Testing Service, 1968.

GOLDMAN, L. *Using Tests in Counseling.* New York: Appleton-Century-Crofts, 1961.

GUILFORD, J. P. *Psychometric Methods.* 2nd ed. New York: McGraw-Hill Book Co., 1954.

LYMAN, H. B. *Test Scores and What They Mean.* Englewood Cliffs, N.J.: Prentice-Hall, Inc., 1963.

POPHAM, W. J., and HUSEK, T. R. "Implications of Criterion-Referenced Measurement," *Journal of Educational Measurement,* Vol. 6 (1969), pp. 1–10.

WESMAN, A. G. *Expectancy Tables—A Way of Interpreting Test Validity.* (Test Service Bulletin No. 38) New York: The Psychological Corporation, 1949.

WESMAN, A. G. *Comparability vs. Equivalence of Test Scores.* (Test Service Bulletin No. 53.) New York: The Psychological Corporation, 1958.

4

CLASSROOM TESTS

The tests used in education can be divided into two broad groups. One group consists of teacher-made *classroom tests*. These tests are constructed by a classroom teacher or several teachers working together, are designed to measure the attainment of the objectives of a particular class or institution, and are usually administered only one time (although individual items may appear on other tests). They may contain one or several types of items—e.g., multiple choice, essay, true-false, completion, problems—and may serve any of a number of purposes. The fact that they are designed to measure the objectives of a specific educational setting is both their strongest point and their major limitation.

The other major class is *standardized tests*. These tests are generally, although not necessarily, constructed by test publishing companies. As they will be used in a wide variety of educational settings, their content reflects, not the objectives of a particular classroom, but generally accepted objectives and materials that are widely taught. Standardized tests are designed jointly by subject matter experts, who are responsible for their content, and test construction experts, who are responsible for technical aspects. Individual items are extensively reviewed and pretested before being included on final forms of the test. Only objectively scorable item types are included (e.g., multiple choice, matching).

The broad content coverage, standardized procedures, and

objective scoring of these tests make them useful instruments for comparing the performance of individuals and groups, as research tools, and as decision-making aids.

The approach to testing described in Chapter 1 would, for the most part, require standardized tests. The reasons are several. First, tests used to make decisions about individuals should attain standards of reliability and validity higher than those generally attained by teacher-made tests. Second, it would be unrealistic to expect the classroom teacher to develop the number and variety of tests needed. Third, differential placement should be based on research evidence; again it would be unrealistic to expect each school system to replicate all studies. Thus data that generalizes across schools is needed; such data would have to come from standardized instruments.

But the approach described in Chapter 1 was more of an ideal, a goal to strive for, than an operational procedure. In the foreseeable future, such an approach will be limited to a few instructional areas. Most educational decision making and instructional planning will be based on the judgment of the classroom teacher and other persons in the local school system. To the extent that they will use test data in making decisions, it will be data from yearly testing programs and classroom tests. Thus the majority of tests that a teacher will use will be his own classroom tests. To better utilize these tests, the teacher should be familiar with the procedures for constructing and analyzing classroom tests. This chapter and the following one will discuss these topics.

Functions of Classroom Tests

Before discussing the planning and construction of classroom tests, we will briefly review some of the functions of classroom tests. Without doubt, the most frequent use of classroom tests is to assess students' mastery of the materials taught in the course. In many circumstances this is but another way of saying that tests are used as a basis for grading; however, there are situations where this knowledge is put to other uses (see below).

Tests are also frequently used to motivate students. Frequently the motivation is negative—the fear of doing poorly on an examination "motivates" a student to study; "pop quizzes" and tests over assignments "motivate" students to keep up-to-date. But as most writers would argue that positive motivation produces more effective learning and less undesirable side effects than negative motivation (see, e.g., Skinner, 1968; Holt, 1964), hopefully, tests would induce positive motivation. The motivating factor usually assumed in education is knowledge of results. Thus, to be maximally effective, test results should be fed back to the student so that he can evaluate his own performance.

Classroom tests also can be used in planning instruction. An obvious example is a pretest, administered prior to an instructional unit to determine students' present level of mastery of the prerequisite skills and/or material to be covered. On any examination, regardless of its purpose, the teacher can determine which items cause difficulty and revise his method of teaching this material. Conversely, items answered correctly by most students generally reflect effective instruction. The general performance level on the test will indicate whether the level of presentation is appropriate.

Teacher-made tests are sometimes used for review, which basically is providing feedback to students regarding their learning. Classroom tests can also serve as a stimulus for discussion, as, for example, when a test is administered and then the reasons for choosing various answers are discussed. The reader can undoubtedly think of other functions of classroom tests.

PLANNING THE TEST

The planning of a classroom test actually begins when the instructor sets the objectives for the course. These objectives will be a function of the instructor's philosophy of education, the goals of the school system or institution, the place of the course in the curriculum, and the instructor's goals for and approach to the particular course. These factors will influence many aspects of examinations: what content is covered, what skills are stressed, the frequency of testing, what purposes tests will be used for, the difficulty of the tests, and so on.

In essence, in education a test will be useful to the extent that it measures whether students have attained the instructional objectives. Hence, unless objectives are clearly specified, there is no way of determining if the test does, in fact, measure attainment of these objectives. Most authorities, therefore, state that objectives should be specified in behavioral terms.

But what precisely does this mean? Mager (1962) has provided guidelines for evaluating the meaningfulness of objectives. He states that an objective should: (1) describe what the learner will be doing when he demonstrates that he has reached the objective, (2) indicate the important conditions and restrictions under which the learner will be expected to demonstrate his competence, (3) indicate how performance will be evaluated, and (4) describe the lower limits of acceptable performance.

Applying these guidelines, the objective of a unit on square roots might be stated: development of the ability to extract square roots of whole numbers, without computational aids, with accuracy to two decimal places, at the rate of one square root per minute.

The Test Plan

The operational vehicle for translating objectives into test items is the *test plan*. A test plan is nothing more than a grid specifying what is to be included within the test. The test items are then written to fit these specifications.

On classroom tests, the plan will usually be two-dimensional, one dimension representing the content covered by the test, the other the skills to be tapped. (Recall that objectives have both content and skill components.) However, other dimensions might be appropriate (for example, on a math test one might plot the types of operation required against the way in which problems are presented—as computations or word problems [ETS, 1961]). Or one might use a large number of dimensions—content, skills, item format, difficulty level. The classroom teacher, however, generally will not need to exceed a two-dimensional plan.

The content dimension generally is easier to define. An outline of the major topics covered is usually available in the teacher's lesson plan, and the reading assignments and source materials used are well specified. Although the latter help define the test coverage (e.g., the exam will cover the syllabus assignments for Unit II plus the materials covered in lectures and discussions on these assignments), the former will be of more use in developing a test plan. To outline the test content the teacher will list 4 to 12 main topics and/or subtopics; these define the content dimension.

Defining the skills dimension is somewhat more difficult. In fact, some authors would argue that one cannot and/or should not even attempt to define a skills dimension. Although the details of their arguments vary, they revolve around two points: (1) content and skills are so inexorably intertwined that any differentiation will be arbitrary, and (2) students may use different skills to solve the same problem. Other persons have attempted to classify the cognitive skills underlying academic performance. In the best known attempt, Bloom *et al.* (1956) developed a *Taxonomy of Educational Objectives*, which included six levels: knowledge, comprehension, application, analysis, synthesis, and evaluation.

The position taken by the author is quite pragmatic. While recognizing that there is some validity to the arguments of critics of the "skill" approach, and finding the *Taxonomy* less than completely useful, as objectives (skills) vary between content areas, we have still found specification of skills to be helpful in planning an exam.

To illustrate how this approach might be used, we have developed a test plan for a unit on test scores in a course on psychological measurement (a unit analogous to parts of Chapter 3 of this book). This plan is presented in Figure 4.1–A. Note that one axis lists the major content headings; the other the skills to be measured. The items constructed following this test plan will not necessarily cover every aspect of the course, but only those which the instructor considers important enough to test.

The test plan in Figure 4.1–A tells what content and skills are to be covered on the test but does not indicate the relative emphasis to be given each topic. Before constructing a test the teacher would, of course, have to decide about relative emphases. Otherwise, he might construct items measuring only one content area or one skill, a procedure that obviously would lead to a poor test.

One frequently used method of determining relative emphases is to weight content and skill categories independently. In Figure 4.1–B, we have assigned weights to each content and skill category. Another instructor teaching the same course and covering the same material might assign different weights; those assigned in Figure 4.1–B were assigned by the test constructor. We could take the assignments of relative emphases one step further by multiplying the weight given each content category by the weight given each skill category, thus obtaining the relative emphasis to be assigned to each content-skill combination. For example, in Figure 4.1–B the topic "percentiles" is weighted 20 percent and "computation" is weighted 30 percent, so items measuring computations of percentile should constitute 6 percent (i.e., $20\% \times 30\% = 6\%$) of the test. To translate these percentages into test score points (or items) we need only multiply the relative weightings by the total number of points (or items) on the test. Thus, if our test was to total 50 points, items covering computations of percentiles would be worth 3 points (i.e., $6\% \times 50$ items).

FIGURE 4.1
A TEST PLAN FOR A UNIT ON TEST SCORES

A. Content and skill categories

Type of Score	Skills			
	Definition	Computation	Interpretation	Evaluation
Raw scores				
Percentiles				
Standard scores				
Developmental scales				
Ratios				
Content scores				

B. Relative weights

Type of Score		Skills			
		Definition 20%	Computation 30%	Interpretation 20%	Evaluation 30%
Raw scores	10%				
Percentiles	20%		20%x30%=6% 6%x50pts=3pts.		
Standard scores	20%				
Developmental scales	20%				
Ratios	10%				
Content scores	20%				

One weakness of this approach is that certain combinations (cells) may not be meaningful (e.g., computation of content scores). However, this method does provide a good approximation, a base from which the test constructor can start.

The reader can best appreciate the problems and procedures in planning a test if he attempts to develop his own test plan. Thus we strongly recommend that before reading further you develop a test plan, either for a topic in a course you are now taking or for a unit in a course in your teaching field. Select the particular unit to be covered, define your objectives for this unit, then write a test plan that reflects this coverage and these objectives.

Item Formats

The test plan indicates the various areas covered and their emphases but does not directly indicate what type nor how many different items will be used. For example, the points devoted to items measuring "computation of percentiles" might all be assigned to one problem or be divided among several short objective items. The teacher must decide which alternative is most appropriate.

Although the teacher can choose from among a wide variety of item types and may want to include several on one exam, a decision often must be made between using a large number of shorter items (e.g., multiple-choice, true-false, completion items) and a smaller number of longer or more comprehensive items (e.g., essay, problems). Using a large number of objective items will result in better sampling of the domain but at the expense of not probing any area in great depth. Conversely, use of a smaller number of broader items allows greater depth of response but sacrifices broad coverage.

Beyond this, the choice of particular item formats will depend on the skills to be tested and the preferences of the teacher. (The advantages and disadvantages of the major item types will be discussed later in the chapter.)

Other Considerations

Planning a test requires making a number of other decisions. We have already alluded to one area, the length of the test. The primary considerations determining length will be the importance of the test and comprehensiveness of coverage desired. Closely related will be the time limits of the test. As indicated previously, unless there is specific reason for using a speed test (such as a typing test), classroom tests generally should allow enough time for everyone to finish.

The difficulty of the test items is also a consideration. It can be shown that if one wants a test to discriminate between individuals, the optimal procedure is to include items that will be correctly answered by about half of the people taking the test. However, for some purposes easy items will suffice—for example, as warm-up items to build confidence or when the purpose of the item is to check if students have done an assignment or understand a concept. Difficult items are useful to separate the very best students from above average students and to test comprehension of complex points.

The teacher must also decide whether students will be allowed to use any aids—for example, slide rules and/or tables in math and science courses. Here the teacher has various alternatives—she can insist that students rely entirely on their memory; she can provide formulae and/or other relevant background information; or she can administer take-home or open-book exams. Proponents of these latter tests stress that they more closely parallel real life than do traditional testing procedures. Furthermore, open-book exams can be designed so that students having the appropriate knowledge in their memory will have an advantage. Take-home exams, of course, allow the student to answer questions in more detail and diminish many of the time pressures. It seems to the author that these types of tests could be utilized more frequently in education.

Finally, when planning a test, the teacher must consider administrative and scoring issues, such as how to record responses and whether to correct scores for guessing. Rather than consider these issues now, we will wait until after we have discussed the various types of items.

ITEM TYPES

Items used on classroom tests can be classified in various ways. For example, certain items are often referred to as objective items —usually in contrast to essay items. But as the term "objective" properly refers to scoring procedures rather than item formats, such a classification is less than perfect. Another common distinction is between recall items (ones which require the student to provide an answer) and recognition items (where he selects between alternative responses). As this classification scheme is based on response processes rather than item formats, it is also unacceptable to some people. They would prefer distinctions such as: (1) supply items—the student "supplies" the response—versus selection items—he "selects" among alternatives or (2) free response versus alternative response. We will distinguish between five classes of item types:

1. *Alternative-choice items*. The student selects a response from a list of possible alternatives; examples include multiple-choice, true-false, and matching items.

2. *Short-answer items*. The student supplies an answer which is only a few words or sentences long; examples include completion, short-answer, identification, and definition items.

3. *Essay questions*. These items require the student to compose a response of some length, usually by culling and integrating materials from a variety of sources.

4. *Problems*. The student must decide on a procedure, then apply it to the solution of the problem posed, usually using data included within the item; most common in mathematics, science, and other quantitative areas.

5. *Performance items*. The student demonstrates his mastery by producing a product or by a nonverbal performance; examples would be demonstrations of athletic skill, musical performances, artistic compositions, and typing tests.

In the following pages we will briefly describe some common item types, consider their advantages and limitations, and discuss variations on the basic formats. Obviously, in such a brief treatment, we cannot discuss the nuances of item construction; the reader who wishes to pursue this topic in more detail should consult Brown (in press) or Ebel (1965).

The reader will better understand and appreciate the material that follows if he can relate it to specific test items. Furthermore, the material will be more meaningful to you if applied to your own teaching field. Thus, rather than providing extensive illustrations of well-constructed and defective items, we would ask you, before reading further in the text, to construct at least 10 multiple-choice items, 10 true-false items, 10 short-answer or completion items, and several matching items. (These might well be items for the exam you have planned previously.) After writing your items, read the sections on alternative-choice and short-answer items. Next, evaluate your items by comparing them to the suggested guidelines for item construction. Then rewrite your items, taking into account the suggestions listed.

ALTERNATIVE-CHOICE ITEMS

Multiple-Choice Items

Multiple-choice items consist of a stem and a small number of alternative responses. Generally the stem will be an incomplete statement or a question; in either case, its function is to clearly state the problem presented by the item. If the stem is an incomplete statement, the alternatives will be phrases that might correctly complete the statement; if the stem is a question, the alternatives will be possible answers to the question. The student may be instructed to select the correct alternative, the incorrect alternative, or the best response to the item.

The typical multiple-choice item contains four or five alternatives; however, with younger children only two to three alternatives may be used. The incorrect alternatives, called *distractors*, should be plausible alternative responses. Distractors usually are selected to represent frequent errors or misunderstandings, superficially similar content, or common misconceptions. (One method of developing distractors is to present the item in short-answer format and use the most frequently given incorrect responses as the distractors.)

Two examples of multiple-choice items are given below.[1] First, from a sixth-grade social studies test:

The Danube River empties into the:
(a) Aegean Sea
(b) Black Sea
(c) Mediterranean Sea

Second, from an examination in an eighth-grade mathematics class:

---

[1] To simplify the discussion and save space, and because the reader can extrapolate from his experience with tests, we will not include directions with our examples nor be concerned with how responses are recorded.

The government has placed a surtax of 10 percent of the basic tax on all income taxes. If the basic tax rate is 25 percent, and Mr. Jones's taxable income is $8,000, his total tax bill will be:

(a) $800   (b) $2,000   (c) $2,200   (d) $2,800

Note that the latter item requires students to apply their knowledge to a practical problem, not just to recall facts. Guidelines for constructing multiple-choice items are given in Exhibit 4.1.

Multiple-choice items can be written for almost any content area. Furthermore, they are not limited to testing factual material; they can measure the ability to apply knowledge, evaluate information, draw conclusions, or solve problems. Scoring is simple, rapid, and objective. Studies have shown that multiple-choice items are usually more reliable and valid than other types of items. As the items are relatively short, many items can be answered in a given time period—usually about one item per minute; therefore, a wide range of content can be sampled by one test.

One limitation is the difficulty of constructing good items. As purely factual items are easiest to construct, many people overemphasize this type of item, thus producing poor tests. Furthermore, constructing plausible alternatives is a difficult task; hence, frequently some responses are obviously wrong and can easily be ignored, thus reducing the difficulty and effectiveness of the item. And, of course, certain skills—e.g., ability to organize material, ability to marshall evidence to support an argument, creativity— cannot be tested using the multiple-choice format. But, by and large, well-constructed multiple-choice items are the best "objective" items, if not the best single type of item.

There are a number of common variations of multiple-choice items. One procedure is to use items where any number of alternatives (including none) may be correct. This format is essentially a cluster true-false item and thus has the advantages and disadvantages of true-false items (see below). Another variation bases several items on a common piece of stimulus material. For example, a reading paragraph, map, graph, or chart may be presented with a series of items based on the information contained therein. This approach can be used when the topic covered merits the emphasis given (i.e., several questions over the same material) and when the questions are independent (i.e., the answer to one item is not dependent on the answer to another in the series). A

EXHIBIT 4.1
GUIDELINES FOR CONSTRUCTING MULTIPLE-CHOICE ITEMS

1. Each item should test one, and only one, central idea.
2. Each item should be independent of every other item; one item should not aid in answering another item.
3. Write as clearly, simply, briefly, and correctly as possible; eliminate all nonfunctional words.
4. Avoid textbook phraseology and examples; whenever feasible, use new situations and terms.
5. The item stem should present the central problem and all qualifications; it should include all words that otherwise would occur in each alternative.
6. Avoid negatively stated items.
7. If an item includes controversial material, cite the authority whose opinion is being used.
8. Alternatives should be homogeneous in content, form, and grammatical structure.
9. There should be one, and only one, correct response; this alternative should be clearly correct.
10. All distractors should be plausible and attractive to students who do not know the correct answer; yet they should be clearly incorrect or inadequate.
11. Distractors may represent common misconceptions, logical alternatives, frequent mistakes, or other plausible but incorrect information.
12. Alternatives should not overlap, include, or be synonymous with each other.
13. Avoid irrelevant clues to the correct response provided by response length, grammar, repetition of key words, common associations, explicitness of response, etc.
14. If alternatives fall in a logical arrangement—e.g., alphabetically, by magnitude—list them in this order.
15. The position of the correct responses should not fall in a pattern but rather be randomized.

third variation is the analogies item. The reader can undoubtedly think of still other possibilities.

True-False Items

Another widely used variety of alternative-choice item is the true-false item. These items consist of a declarative statement which the student judges either true or false (or by a similar distinction such as correct-incorrect). Typical items would be:

T F The Danube River empties into the Mediterranean Sea.

T F If a 10 percent surtax is added to all income taxes, and the basic tax rate is 25 percent, Mr. Jones, whose taxable income is $8,000, will have a total tax bill of $2,800.

(Compare the same questions expressed in the multiple-choice format above.) True-false items are best suited to presenting unambiguous factual material and for testing younger children who will not be misled by subtle phrasing and nuances in the item.

EXHIBIT 4.2

GUIDELINES FOR CONSTRUCTING TRUE-FALSE ITEMS

1. Items should deal with a single idea, not a combination of several ideas.
2. Express each item simply and clearly in words whose meanings are definite and precise; include no more than one qualifying phrase.
3. Statements should be entirely true or entirely false, not partially true and partially false.
4. The crucial element in the statement should be apparent to the student; the truth of the statement should not rest on trivial details or trick phrases.
5. Items should be based on significant facts, principles and generalizations.
6. Include approximately equal numbers of true and false items on the test; make sure correct responses do not fall in a pattern.
7. Whenever possible, use quantitative rather than qualitative terminology.
8. Do not create false statements by inserting "not" into true statements.
9. Avoid mere repetition of textbook statements and statements that are minor variations of textbook statements.
10. Avoid specific determiners—i.e., words like sometimes, never, always—that may provide clues to the correctness of the statement.
11. When items refer to controversial material or to matters of opinion or value, cite the authority whose opinion is being used.

(Some guidelines for constructing true-false items are presented in Exhibit 4.2.) True-false items share many of the advantages of alternative-choice items—they can be scored rapidly and objectively, can be subjected to item analysis, and permit wide content sampling. Being shorter than multiple-choice items, more true-false items can be presented in a given time period. In addition, true-false items are easier to construct than multiple-choice items.

Their major limitations are that they are restricted to testing unambiguous factual materials, that they force the student to make an absolute judgment of the truth of a statement, and that subtle changes in wording are likely to have significant effects on the meaning of the items. As there are only two possible responses, reliability may be lowered and guessing can play a large role. For these reasons, most test constructors prefer multiple-choice to true-false items.

Several format variations are possible. A cluster true-false item contains a stem followed by several alternatives, the student's task being to indicate whether each alternative produces a true or a false statement. This item type is identical to multiple-choice items that allow more than one correct response. Another variation is to ask the student to judge the truth or falsity of each statement, and if the item is false, explain why it is false. Also, some persons have attempted to increase the reliability and validity of true-false items by having the student respond using more than two categories (e.g., true, probably true, probably false, false) or by indicating their degree of confidence in the truth or falsity of each statement. These attempts have met with mixed success.

Matching Items

A matching item is essentially a series of multiple-choice items, each having a common set of alternatives. The item consists of two parallel lists: one containing stimulus words or phrases, the other response alternatives. The student's task is to match the terms on the two lists. Matching items should contain no more than five to eight stimuli, with slightly more responses. Each response may be used only once or more than once, depending on the directions.

The most critical consideration in matching items is that the content be homogeneous. For example, the item below requires matching common abbreviations with their translation:

(1) e.g.	(a) note well, consider carefully
(2) i.e.	(b) for example
(3) etc.	(c) at or about the time of
(4) et al.	(d) and others
(5) n.b.	(e) and so forth
	(f) that is

A common error in constructing matching items is to include heterogeneous content in one or both lists. This allows students to cluster responses and eliminate some responses as being obviously inappropriate. For example, if a single matching item on a history test required the matching of persons and places to their descriptions, when considering an alternative dealing with a person the student could disregard all responses referring to places, thus reducing the number of possible correct responses to be considered.

Another common error is to include a large number of terms in each list. This procedure will either result in heterogeneous items or place undue emphasis on one topic. It also results in disproportionate amounts of time being spent searching among alternatives, time that better could be spent evaluating responses.

Matching items share the rapid and objective scoring features of alternative-choice items. They also are more efficient than multiple-choice items, as they avoid repetition of alternatives. Conversely, when using a matching question, the teacher must decide whether she really wants to devote so much emphasis to a particular content area or type of item. Unfortunately, as it is easiest to construct matching items which cover factual material, matching items are often restricted to testing factual memory.

SHORT-ANSWER ITEMS

Some people object to alternative-response items because they only require students to select among given alternatives or to recognize correct and incorrect statements. They feel that a more demanding task would be for the student to recall and supply a correct answer. Short-answer items provide an item format that meets some of these objections.

The skills and content measured by an alternative-choice item can, in general, also be evaluated by one or more type of short-answer item. For example, as short-answer items our two examples might be phrased:

Into what sea does the Danube River empty? _____
_____

If a 10 percent surtax is added to all income taxes, and the basic tax rate is 25 percent, how much income tax will Mr. Jones, whose taxable income is $8,000, have to pay?
$_____

And as completion items:

The Danube River empties into the _____ Sea.

If a 10 percent surtax is added to all income taxes, and the basic tax rate is 25 percent, Mr. Jones, whose taxable income is $8,000, will have to pay $_____ in income taxes.

As the same material can be tested by several formats, other considerations than item format will determine how the item is presented.

Types of Short-Answer Items

The specific item type referred to as a *short-answer* item consists of a question to which the student responds in a word, phrase, or at most, one or two sentences. The first two examples above illustrated the format, as do the following items:

List three characteristics of birds.
   1. _____
   2. _____
   3. _____

What was the major campaign issue in the presidential election of 1860? _____

Who developed the first individual intelligence test?
_____

Although short-answer items are applicable in a wide range of content and skills areas, they are particularly appropriate when the educational goal is for the student to be able to recall or identify names, formulae, or terms; to list distinguishing features; or to classify objects, terms, or events.

A closely related type is the *completion* item, which differs primarily in the fact that the answer completes the item statement. That is, the typical completion item consists of a statement with one or several crucial words or phrases deleted; the student's task is to supply the missing words so as to correctly complete the sentence. Two examples were given above; others would be:

Smaller towns near large cities are called _____.

The 14 main divisions of animal life are called _____

_____.

In psychological testing, the consistency with which a test measures is called _____ and the degree to which a test measures what it is designed to measure is called _____.

Like short-answers items, the student must recall and supply the correct responses. Again, the format is appropriate for testing in most content areas.

A *definition* item requires the student to define a word, term, or formula. Frequently a limitation is placed on the length of the response, say: define the terms in a sentence. Definition items are obviously appropriate whenever mastery of terminology is an important educational goal. Variations on the format are also possible. For example, rather than defining a term, the student might be

---

EXHIBIT 4.3

GUIDELINES FOR CONSTRUCTING SHORT-
ANSWER ITEMS

1. Try to phrase items so that there is only one possible correct response.
2. Phrase items so that the student is clear what type of response is demanded; that is, so he knows the length and preciseness of response required, or, in an item with a numerical response, the units in which the answer should be expressed.
3. The response, preferably, should be a single word or short phrase.
4. Avoid using statements taken directly from the text.
[Rules 5–7 apply to completion items.]
5. Omit only key words, not trivia.
6. Place the blank near the end of the sentence.
7. Avoid overmutilated items; include a maximum of two blanks within an item.

---

asked to indicate the importance of a term, concept, person, place, or event, or he might be asked to translate a foreign word or phrase into English (or vice versa) or give a verbal equivalent of a mathematical formula.

Identification items are distinguished by using something other than a verbal statement as the stimulus. For example, students might be presented with a chart, map, or graph and asked to identify designated points. Or various rock samples might be displayed and students asked to identify or classify each specimen. Or a plant or animal specimen might be displayed, with students to identify various organs. Needless to say, such items can readily be expanded beyond simple identification to include questions about the identified part; for example, students may be asked to describe its function or importance.

Some guidelines for constructing short-answer items are given in Exhibit 4.3.

Advantages and Limitations

As short-answer and alternative-choice items are generally interchangeable in terms of coverage of content and skill domains, the choice between the two formats will rest on other considerations. What, then, are the advantages and limitations of short-answer items, and how do they compare to alternative-choice items?

Like alternative-choice items, short-answer items are relatively brief; thus, wide content sampling is possible within short time limits. In addition, many teachers find short-answer items easier to construct than multiple-choice items because they do not have to develop plausible distractors. As the response process is more straightforward and less confusing, short-answer items may be more appropriate for younger children. Because students must supply answers, guessing is minimized.

Although the scoring of short-answer items is more objective than the scoring of essay, problem, and performance items, it is not as objective as the scoring of alternative-choice items. Thus the teacher (or other scorer) will often have to decide how much credit to allow for an answer. For example, one frequently encounters misspellings. Suppose, in response to the question, "Who developed the first individual intelligence test?" a student writes "Benet." Should the teacher grant full credit for this answer, ignoring the misspelling of Binet; or should the student receive only partial credit; or should the answer be counted as incorrect? It is easy to see that more complex items requiring longer answers (e.g., definitions) would require even more judgments by the scorer. Thus scoring problems—both the lack of objectivity and the increased time needed for scoring—are the greatest technical drawback of short-answer items.

In summary, short-answer items are usually interchangeable with alternative items. Their simpler response format makes them more appropriate than alternative-choice items for young children. Although they are easier and less time-consuming to construct, this advantage is counterbalanced by longer and less objective scoring. The decision whether to use short-answer or alternative-choice items, thus, will usually hinge on two factors: (1) whether the teacher wants to stress recall rather than recognition, and (2) whether use of one or the other item formats allows her to construct better items. Of course, there is no reason why both formats cannot be used, either on the same examination or on separate examinations.

ESSAY QUESTIONS

One of the perennial controversies in educational testing concerns the relative merits of essay and objective[2] tests. While test construction experts generally prefer to use objective items because of their technical superiority, many educators and critics of education favor essay examinations. In fact, many persons vehemently decry the use of objective tests in education. (The reader who is interested in this controversy should read Hoffman, 1961, 1962; Black, 1963; and Chauncey and Dobbin, 1963.)

You are all familiar with essay questions. They consist of a statement, usually several sentences long, that sets a problem; the student then composes an "essay" as an answer to the problem. This answer may be as brief as a paragraph or may be several pages in length.

Many other types of evaluation procedures—e.g., themes, written reports, and book reviews—are essentially variations of essay exams. In many ways, problems (see below) also can be considered variations of essay questions. Other procedures, like take-

---

[2] When being compared to essay tests, the term "objective" may include both alternative-choice and short-answer items or, more commonly, only alternative-choice items. However, we will generally use the term in the broader sense.

home exams, do not change the item content or format but, by reducing time pressures, eliminate the effects of some irrelevant variables.

Stecklein (1955) has listed the abilities and objectives most often measured by essay questions. These include: (1) comparisons between two or more things, (2) the development and defense of an opinion, (3) questions of cause and effect, (4) explanations of meanings, (5) summarizing of information in a designated area, (6) analysis, (7) knowledge of relationships, (8) illustrations of rules, principles, procedures, and applications, (9) applications of rules, laws, and principles to new situations, (10) criticisms of the adequacy, relevance, or correctness of a concept, idea, or information, (11) formulation of new questions and problems, (12) reorganizations of facts, (13) discriminations between objects, concepts, or events, and (14) inferential thinking.

Advantages

The advantages stressed by proponents of essay exams are that they require the student to compose his own answer, rather than select among given alternatives; that writing an acceptable essay requires the student to utilize certain skills—e.g., organizational ability, integration, evaluation, summarization, writing ability— which cannot be tested by other items; that the essay format is flexible; and that a topic can be probed in depth, with the student being able to explain and defend his reasoning. Many persons would also feel that essay exams are easier to construct than objective items. Finally, only open-ended items, such as essays, provide an opportunity for the student to display his creativity, originality, and ability to think divergently.

Limitations

There are several problems with essay questions. First, although many persons feel that essay examinations are easier to construct than objective exams, this feeling may be more illusory than real. A good essay question treads a thin line between being so general that the problem is not really defined and being so specific that it is little more than a series of short-answer items. (See Exhibit 4.4 for suggestions regarding the construction of essay questions.)

EXHIBIT 4.4
GUIDELINES FOR CONSTRUCTING ESSAY QUESTIONS

1. The question should clearly and unambiguously define the task for the student, but without interfering with the measurement of the intended outcomes.
2. The question should indicate the direction and scope of answer desired.
3. The question should require the student to demonstrate his command of essential background knowledge.
4. Use questions that have clearly acceptable correct answers, rather than ones that only measure opinions or attitudes.
5. It is usually better to use more specific questions which can be answered briefly rather than fewer broad, general questions.
6. Do not use optional questions.
7. Start essay questions with phrases such as: compare and contrast, present the arguments for and against, give the reasons for, explain how (or why), give an example of, and so on.

Second, as a longer time is required to compose and write an answer to an essay question,[3] only a few questions may be included in any examination. Thus sampling adequacy and content coverage are usually sacrificed. Although some instructors dismiss the objection, saying that a good student should know "everything" about a subject and thus will not be penalized, such a view of learning and evaluation is quite naive.

Third, irrelevant variables—e.g., writing speed, verbal facility, and writing style—can affect responses. And, although it may appear on first blush that essay questions are not susceptible to faking, in many instances one can easily bluff his way through an essay question.

But perhaps the central problem with essay questions concerns scoring. It should be obvious that scoring essay exams is a time-consuming process. In fact, any time saved during test construction is more than compensated for by the additional scoring time. Furthermore, it is a well documented fact that the scoring of essay exams is notoriously unreliable. Even when precautions are taken to increase scoring reliability (see Chapter 5), there still often will be wide differences between the scores assigned to the same paper

---

[3] In the author's experience, few essay questions can be adequately answered by high school or college students in less than 30 minutes, with more time per item being preferable. Thus, I now give essay questions only as take-home exams.

EXHIBIT 4.5

COMPARISON OF ESSAY AND OBJECTIVE TESTS

	Essay	Objective
Abilities Measured	Requires the student to express himself in his own words, using information from his own background and knowledge.	Requires the student to select correct answers from given options, or to supply an answer limited to one word or phrase.
	Can tap high levels of reasoning such as required in inference, organization of ideas, comparison and contrast.	Can *also* tap high levels of reasoning such as required in inference, organization of ideas, comparison and contrast.
	Does *not* measure purely factual information efficiently.	Measures knowledge of facts efficiently.
Scope	Covers only a limited field of knowledge in any one test. Essay questions take so long to answer that relatively few can be answered in a given period of time. Also, the student who is especially fluent can often avoid discussing points of which he is unsure.	Covers a broad field of knowledge in one test. Since objective questions may be answered quickly, one test may contain many questions. A broad coverage helps provide reliable measurement.
Incentive to Pupils	Encourages pupils to learn how to organize their own ideas and express them effectively.	Encourages pupils to build up a broad background of knowledge and abilities.
Ease of Preparation	Requires writing only a few questions for a test. Tasks must be clearly defined, general enough to offer some leeway, specific enough to set limits.	Requires writing many questions for a test. Wording must avoid ambiguities and "giveaways." Distractors should embody most likely misconceptions.
Scoring	Usually very time-consuming to score. Permits teachers to comment directly on the reasoning processes of individual pupils. However, an answer may be scored differently by different teachers or by the same teacher at different times.	Can be scored quickly. Answer generally scored only right or wrong, but scoring is very accurate and consistent.

Source: *Making the Classroom Test: A Guide for Teachers.* Copyright © 1959 by Educational Testing Service. All rights reserved. Reprinted by permission.

by different graders and/or the scores assigned by the same grader on two separate scorings.

Thus when deciding whether to use essay questions, the teacher must decide if the advantages of measuring certain skills which are not tested by other items outweigh the disadvantages of restricted content sampling and scoring problems. Exhibit 4.5 summarizes this problem by comparing essay and objective items.

PROBLEMS AND PERFORMANCE ITEMS

Finally, we will briefly discuss problems and performance items. Our brevity should not be taken as an index of the relative importance of these types of items. These items are more directly tied to particular content areas and, in a brief book, we do not have space to consider each of the myriad of possible areas.

Problems

In many ways, problems serve the same function in the sciences and mathematics as essay questions do in nonquantitative areas. The problem item is likely to be quite similar to an essay question, presenting some problem for the student to solve. In contrast to an essay question, however, a problem will frequently contain some (quantitative) data to be manipulated. Although the student's task will vary, depending on the subject matter, an identifiable sequence of steps usually is involved: (1) the student must identify the problem or basic question asked, (2) he must also identify the relevant data and parameters, (3) he must set up an equation or an operational procedure, (4) he must apply this equation or procedure to the relevant data in order to arrive at a solution. Problems are particularly appropriate for testing whether students understand principles and whether they can apply these principles to new data and situations.

The construction and scoring of problems is analogous to essay questions. As with essay questions, many of the limitations appear in scoring. Although problems may appear to have only one solution, often several solutions are possible. Furthermore, the student will frequently be correct in some aspects of his solution but not in others—for example, he may set up the correct equation but use inappropriate data or make a computational error. As use of all-or-none scoring procedures throws away too much valuable data, the scorer will constantly be faced with decisions about how much credit to award the student for a partially correct answer.

It should also be noted that many problems, particularly shorter ones, can also be cast as multiple-choice or true-false items. In fact, one of our examples (see above) illustrates this clearly.

Even more so than problems, performance items are specific to content areas. As mentioned above, a performance item requires the student to make something, perform, or demonstrate a skill. In some instances, such as typing tests, performance can be evaluated objectively—e.g., in terms of "words typed per minute." In most situations, however, the evaluation of the performance will be a rating by the teacher or other expert judge. Rather than discuss rating problems here, we will postpone our discussion to Chapter 8.

ASSEMBLING AND ADMINISTERING THE TEST

After the test items have been written, the teacher can assemble the final form of the test. Before doing this, however, he should check to insure that the distribution of items, by content/skill categories, parallels that outlined in the test plan. As certain types of items usually will be easier to write, the teacher will frequently find that some content/skill areas are overrepresented and others underrepresented by the items. Thus he may have to delete some items and/or write additional items to attain adequate content sampling. Once this is obtained, the test can be assembled. As this task is based on common sense and has no set rules, we will mention only a few of the most important considerations.

Test items can be presented to students in various ways. The optimal procedure is to duplicate the items so that each student will have his own copy of the test. Other possibilities include writing the items on the chalkboard (if the test is short), presenting the questions orally, and projecting items onto a screen. Regardless of how the test is presented, the overriding consideration is that each student has clear and ready access to all needed materials. This is particularly important if graphs, tables, diagrams, or similar materials are included on the test. Students may respond on the test itself or on separate answer sheets. With younger (elementary school) children responding on the test itself is preferable. Although this procedure may increase scoring time slightly, it will avoid confusion in responding.

As with mode of presentation, there are few definitive rules for ordering items within tests. Many teachers like to begin with several easy items so students will not become discouraged or sidetracked by hard questions at the beginning of the test. If the test contains several item types, the shorter items (e.g., multiple-choice, true-false, completion) should come before problems and essay questions. All materials related to a single question, or group of questions, should be placed on the same page (so that students do not have to keep turning between pages). If the test items fall in some logical or topical arrangement, they can be presented in this order; otherwise a random arrangement will suffice.

What directions need to be included will depend on the composition of the class, particularly their familiarity with the types of items on the test. As most item formats used on classroom tests are familiar to students, minimal directions will usually suffice. The student should know how to indicate his answer and, on free response items, the length or depth of answer required. The time limits, any instructions regarding guessing, and the amount of credit awarded for each item (or type of item) should be stated, either on the test or orally. Of course, the teacher should answer any questions, before or during the examination, regarding procedures. He should also check during the examination to see that all students are responding properly.

Unless the test requires special displays, equipment, or procedures, it can be administered as part of the regular classroom routine. All exams should, of course, be scheduled when there is sufficient time for students to complete the test, at a logical place within the instructional sequence, and so that distractions are minimized (for example, do not schedule an exam just prior to a vacation or immediately after a pep assembly.)

The philosophy of the author is that students should always be given sufficient advance notice, not only of the exact time when a test will be given but also of what content the test will cover and of what format the items will take. This announcement allows students to prepare to the extent that *they* desire. If "pop quizzes" or unscheduled examinations are a necessary or desirable part of the course, the teacher should inform the students, at the beginning of the term, that such quizzes will occur periodically.

Finally there is the question of test anxiety. Some students get so tense when taking examinations that their performance is adversely affected. Mild cases of test anxiety often can be alleviated by insuring that students are thoroughly familiar with the testing procedures and know what material will be covered on the exam (see previous paragraph). More intense cases may require special testing arrangements or counseling.

SUMMARY

Most of the tests that teachers use are their own classroom tests, not standardized tests. This chapter discussed the planning and construction of these teacher-made tests.

The first step in developing classroom tests is the setting of the course objectives. These objectives are translated into a prescription for a particular test through a test plan. A test plan indicates what content and skills are to be covered by the examination and the relative emphases to be given each content/skill category. Items are then written to sample the specific content/skill areas listed in the plan.

The bulk of the chapter was devoted to a discussion of five types of test items—alternative-choice items, short-answer items, essay questions, problems, and performance items—with emphasis on the first three classes. The skills tested, uses, and advantages and limitations of each type were presented, and the relative merits of alternative-choice and short-answer items and of objective and essay items were compared.

The procedures for administering classroom tests were discussed briefly.

REFERENCES

BLACK, H. *They Shall Not Pass.* New York: William Morrow & Co., Inc., 1963.

BLOOM, B. S., *et al. Taxonomy of Educational Objectives.* (Handbook I, *Cognitive Domain.*) New York: David McKay Co., Inc., 1956.

BROWN, F. G. *Measuring Achievement in the Classroom.* Hinsdale, Ill.: The Dryden Press, in press.

CHAUNCEY, H., and DOBBIN, J. E. *Testing: Its Place in Education Today.* New York: Harper & Row, Publishers, 1963.

EBEL, R. L. *Measuring Educational Achievement.* Englewood Cliffs, N.J.: Prentice-Hall, Inc., 1965.

EDUCATIONAL TESTING SERVICE. *Making the Classroom Test: A Guide for Teachers.* (Evaluation and Advisory Service Series No. 4.) Princeton, N.J., 1961.

HOFFMAN, B. "The Tyranny of Multiple-Choice Tests," *Harper's Magazine,* March, 1961, pp. 37–44.

HOFFMAN, B. *The Tyranny of Testing.* New York: Crowell Collier and Macmillan, Inc., 1962.

HOLT, J. *How Children Fail.* New York: Pitman Publishing Corp., 1964.

MAGER, R. F. *Preparing Objectives for Programmed Instruction.* San Francisco: Fearon Publishers, Inc., 1962.

SKINNER, B. F. *The Technology of Teaching.* New York: Appleton-Century-Crofts, 1968.

STECKLEIN, J. E. *Essay Tests: Why and How?* (University of Minnesota, Bureau of Institutional Research, Bulletin on Classroom Testing No. 2.) Minneapolis, 1955.

5

ANALYZING TEST SCORES AND ITEMS

After administering a classroom examination the next step is to score the test papers. In most cases, scoring the tests and recording the scores (usually for future use in determining grades) completes the teacher's concern with the test. But, if we want to make maximum use of the information contained in classroom tests, we can further analyze the items and test scores. These analyses are designed to indicate: (1) how the class performed on the test as a whole and on the individual items and (2) how successful instruction was and how it might be improved.

In this chapter we will consider procedures for analyzing test scores and individual test items. Although our discussion will be directed toward the classroom test, many of the same procedures will be applicable to standardized tests. But first we will devote a few pages to test scoring.

SCORING

The process of scoring a test actually begins during the construction phase. While building test items, the teacher must decide on both the correct response and the relative weight to be assigned each item. Furthermore, if an item permits alternative responses or partial solutions (for example, as do essay items and problems) he must decide what alternative approaches will be acceptable and the proportional credit to be assigned each response variation. Failure to consider these problems during test construction may result in unanswerable items appearing on the test or in unanticipated scoring problems.

Scoring involves three distinct steps. First, the students' responses must be recorded, preferably completely and unambiguously. On alternative-choice items the student will indicate the letter or number of the correct alternative (e.g., by circling T or F on a true-false item). On short-answer items, he will fill in the blanks or write the necessary phrases or sentences. On essay questions the response, of course, will be the completed essay. And, on problems, it will generally be the step-by-step indication of the procedure followed. Responses may be recorded either on the test or on separate answer sheets. The former procedure, answering on the test, is particularly recommended when testing younger children. In any case, unless answers are completely and unambiguously recorded, the teacher will not be able to score the test accurately.

Second, the teacher must develop a list of correct responses, acceptable variations, and scoring weights; this is the *scoring key.* As indicated above, the teacher should develop this key during test construction in order to anticipate any scoring problems.

Third, students' responses must be compared to the key. As there is only one acceptable correct answer for each item, scoring alternative-choice items involves only comparing students' responses to the key. If students respond on the test, scoring may be done by a visual comparison or by using an overlay or scoring stencil; if separate answer sheets are used, tests may also be scored by electronic scoring machines.

A question that may arise when scoring alternative-choice items is whether to apply a *correction for guessing.* Some persons feel that the alternative-choice format allows students to spuriously inflate their scores by guessing when uncertain of the correct response (see, e.g., Davis, 1951, 1964). Thus they advocate applying a correction formula:

$$X_{\text{corr}} = R - \frac{W}{n-1} \qquad (5.1)$$

where $X_{\text{corr}} =$ the corrected score, $R =$ the number of correct responses, $W =$ the number of wrong answers, and $n =$ the number of alternatives per item; omitted items are not considered. Applied to true-false items the formula becomes:

$$X_{corr} = R - W \qquad (5.1a)$$

and for a four-alternative multiple-choice item the formula would be:

$$X_{corr} = R - \frac{W}{3} \qquad (5.1b)$$

Other authors (e.g., Ebel, 1965) feel that as there is no evidence that corrected scores are more accurate than uncorrected scores and applying the correction involves additional computations, the correction is superfluous. The present author subscribes to this latter view. However, if the teacher wishes to discourage or penalize guessing, he can apply the correction. Students, of course, should be informed if the correction will be applied.

Scoring short-answer items is somewhat more complex, as alternative correct answers are possible on many items. Thus the teacher should develop a schedule which indicates the amount of credit to be given for each possible response, using guidelines that allow consistent scoring from item to item. (Good examples can be found in the scoring manuals for the Stanford-Binet and Wechsler intelligence scales.) Even with these scoring guides, unanticipated responses will frequently occur, requiring the teacher to make decisions regarding the score to be assigned to the response.

Essay and problem items present many of the same problems, only in greater complexity because of the increased length of response. On these items, scoring problems can be minimized by adopting certain rules:

1. Items should be phrased so that students will use the same approach, rather than producing widely divergent responses.
2. Prepare a model answer. This model should include the major topics to be covered and the points to be awarded for inclusion, or omission, of each topic.
3. Grade the tests item by item, rather than person by person.
4. The student whose paper is being scored should be anonymous.
5. If possible, grade all examinations, or a sample of them, twice to check the consistency of scoring. If possible, have the same item graded by several scorers.

These procedures, while not eliminating scorer unreliability, should decrease variability (increase consistency) and thus produce more accurate and fairer scores.

Here, again, the reader will profit from actually trying out the suggestions made in the text. For example, prepare an essay question and administer it to several students. Then have the responses graded by two sets of graders: one group using only their own judgment and a second group utilizing a model answer. The discrepancies between graders and the differences in the variability of grades assigned under the two procedures should illustrate the problems involved in grading essay exams.

The scoring weight assigned to any item will depend on the relative emphasis the teacher wants to place on that item. Generally weights will be proportional to the amount of time the student devotes to answering the item. Unless there is some compelling argument for doing otherwise, alternative-choice and short-answer items usually will be worth one point per item and credit for other items will be scaled in relation to these items.[1]

ANALYZING TEST SCORES

After all items have been scored, each student's scores on the individual items are usually summed to obtain his total or raw score on the test. These raw scores may be analyzed further to provide information regarding: (1) the test itself, (2) the students' level of mastery of the material covered by the test, and (3) students' relative performance. In this section we will focus on the first two uses; the third will be discussed in Chapter 8.

Describing Score Distributions

To illustrate how scores might be analyzed, assume that a 20-item multiple-choice test was administered to a class of 40 students. The scores were:

```
10  16  12  14  15   9  20  14  13  16  17  13  11  16
14  18  14  15  12  15  15  17  11  13  19  12  14  14
    10  11  19  12  15  13  17  13  16   8  14  18
```

---

[1] The absolute values used in any given set of scoring weights are, of course, arbitrary, as scores can be transformed to various scales. Thus the important consideration will be the relative weights given each item or section of the test.

These scores, as they stand, tell us little—only that there are 40 scores, and that the highest score attained was 20 and the lowest was 8.

We would have a clearer picture of the distribution of scores if they were arranged in a *frequency distribution,* which is a tabulation of the frequency (f) with which each score (X) occurs. The procedures for developing a frequency distribution are shown in Exhibit 5.1. This frequency distribution shows clearly that the

---

EXHIBIT 5.1   )

DEVELOPMENT OF A FREQUENCY DISTRIBUTION

To develop a frequency distribution:

1. List all possible scores in order of magnitude.
2. Tally the frequency of occurrence of each score.
3. The number of tallies for each score is that score's frequency; the sum of the frequencies will equal the total number of scores in the set.

Score X	Tally	Frequency f
20	/	1
19	//	2
18	//	2
17	///	3
16	////	4
15	ЖНL	5
14	ЖНL //	7
13	ЖНL	5
12	////	4
11	///	3
10	//	2
9	/	1
8	/	1
		40

---

scores tend to bunch up in the middle ranges (around a score of 14) and that extremely high and low scores occur less frequently. These relationships could also be shown graphically, as a frequency polygon, by plotting the scores against the relative frequencies (see Figure 5.1).

Some other common test score distributions are shown in Figure 5.2. Distribution A is the bell-shaped *normal distribution.* Although the normal distribution is a mathematical concept, and thus test scores never fall into a perfectly normal distribution, most standardized tests are constructed so that the obtained score distribution will approximate a normal distribution, as it can be shown that maximal discrimination between individuals will occur with this distribution. Distribution B is a *negatively skewed distribution;* here many people obtain high scores with scores tailing-off

FIGURE 5.1

A FREQUENCY POLYGON

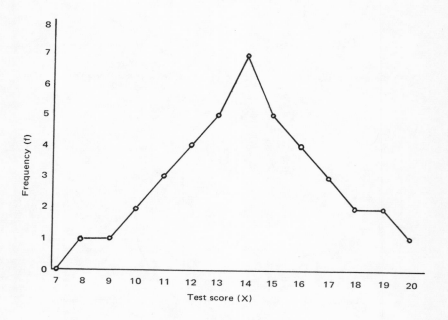

Note: This figure is a plot of the score distribution given in the text example and in Exhibit 5.1.

toward the low end of the range. This distribution will be obtained when the test is easy (i.e., many people obtain high scores) and thus may be desirable on tests designed to measure mastery of a unit, to check if an assignment had been read, or to identify persons needing remedial work. Distribution C, in contrast, is a *positively skewed distribution,* with most persons obtaining quite low scores. This distribution would result from a difficult test and would be appropriate when maximum discrimination is desired among persons with high degrees of knowledge, for example, on a

FIGURE 5.2
EXAMPLES OF TEST SCORE DISTRIBUTIONS

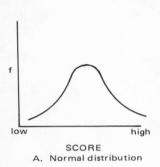

A. Normal distribution

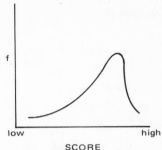

B. Negatively skewed distribution

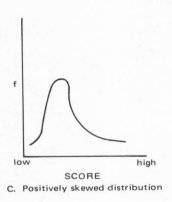

C. Positively skewed distribution

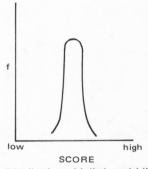

D. Distribution with little variability

test used for awarding scholarships or when selecting students for an advanced or accelerated section of a course. Distribution D shows a test with *distribution with little variability,* one where most students obtain about the same score. Such a distribution obviously allows little discrimination between individuals.

In many situations it is desirable to have a single value that summarizes the average performance of the group, a measure of *central tendency.* Three measures are commonly used. The *mode* is the score that occurs with the greatest frequency—in our example, 14 is the modal score, as more people obtained a score of 14 than any other score. The *median* is the score above and below which half of the group fall; in our example the median[2] also is 14. The most useful measure of central tendency is the arithmetic average, or *mean*, which is defined as the sum of the scores divided by the number of scores:

$$\bar{X} = \frac{\Sigma X}{n} \qquad (5.2)$$

where $\bar{X}$ = the mean, Σ means "the sum of" and n = the number of scores. In our example:

$$\Sigma X = 10 + 16 + 12 + \ldots + 14 + 18 = 565$$

and, therefore, the mean is:

$$\bar{X} = \frac{\Sigma X}{n} = \frac{565}{40} = 14.1$$

The mean and other measures of central tendency tell us the average score but do not indicate how widely scores vary around this average. As distributions can vary not only in average score but also in *variability* (compare Figures 5.2–A and 5.2–D), to describe a distribution we also need an index of variability. The most common one is the *standard deviation:*

$$s = \sqrt{\frac{\Sigma x^2}{n}} = \sqrt{\frac{\Sigma(X - \bar{X})^2}{n}} \qquad (5.3)$$

where s = the standard deviation and $x = X - \bar{X}$, the deviation of a score from the mean. Thus, s is a measure of average variability of scores from the mean. Using the data from our example:

$$\Sigma x^2 = (10 - 14.1)^2 + (16 - 14.1)^2 + \ldots + (18 - 14.1)^2 = 307.6$$

and

$$s = \sqrt{307.6/40} = \sqrt{7.69} = 2.8$$

---

[2] There are several alternative methods for deriving each of the statistics that we will be illustrating. However, as our purpose is not to teach statistics, we will use simple methods in our examples. For other methods see any statistics book, e.g., Edwards, 1969.

The mean gives an indication of the difficulty of the test; the standard deviation indicates how widely the scores varied around the mean. These two values can be used: (1) to describe performance on a particular test—in our example, the average student correctly answered 70 percent of the items, (2) to compare several tests—e.g., to determine their relative difficulty or variability, (3) to interpret the score of an individual on a particular test—in our example, a person scoring 17 was approximately one standard deviation above the mean, and (4) as a basis for comparing an individual's relative performance on several tests.

Consistency

As the teacher generally builds but one form of a test and administers it only one time, a measure of consistency may seem superfluous; that is, the teacher will use the test, regardless of whether or not it measures consistently. Yet, to insure that the test measures achievement at better than a chance level, and as an aid in building future tests, the teacher may want to investigate the consistency with which her test measures. The fact that only one form of the test is available and that the test is administered only once eliminates the possibility of using measures of stability or equivalence. Thus the teacher will have to use either a split-half estimate or a measure of internal consistency (see Chapter 2).

The split-half reliability coefficient, you will recall, represents the correlation between scores on two halves of the test—usually scores on the odd-numbered items and on the even-numbered items. If the test measures consistently, the correlation between the two halves should be high. If the correlation is low, the test may be measuring inconsistently or some artifact in the split of items may have produced the low correlation. An example of the computation of a split-half reliability coefficient is shown in Exhibit 5.2.

The other possible index is a measure of internal consistency, such as Kuder-Richardson formula 20. As the computational labor is tedious, use of this technique is usually infeasible unless computational aids are available. Furthermore, the formula assumes that all items measure the same skill or ability—that is, that the test is homogeneous. As classroom tests usually measure diverse content and skills (i.e., are heterogeneous), the formula may not be completely applicable and the consistency of the scores may be underestimated. If data processing equipment is readily available, more sophisticated measures of reliability—e.g., Cronbach's coefficient alpha, average interitem correlations (see Chapter 2)—can be computed.

As we have stated in the previous paragraph, computation of reliability indices is tedious, and unless the teacher has access to automated scoring and/or computing services, he probably will not routinely compute these indices. However, the teacher should periodically compute a consistency estimate for one of his tests, if only to remind himself that his tests are far from perfect measuring instruments.

Validity

The goal of educational measurement is to develop valid tests. On achievement tests, content validity will be the most important consideration, the best test being one that most adequately samples the relevant content domain. Thus the most important evidence of the validity of a classroom test will be obtained from a thorough item-by-item comparison of the test to the test plan and course goals. To the extent that the test representatively samples these goals, it will be a valid test.

In some situations, additional validity evidence can be obtained by comparing the test scores to some outside criterion. For example, within the class the teacher may compare scores on a test to scores on another examination, to performance on other class assignments, or to her ratings of the students' comprehension of the course material. If the course is part of a sequence of courses, test scores can be compared with performance in the following course. Scores on classroom tests can be compared to scores on standardized achievement tests used by the school. It is important to remember, however, that each type of performance may involve different skills and thus performance on separate measures will not necessarily be highly correlated. However, if there is little relationship between scores on our classroom tests and these other measures, we should question whether our classroom tests really are measuring important skills.

EXHIBIT 5.2

COMPUTATION OF A SPLIT-HALF RELIABILITY COEFFICIENT

Computation of a split-half reliability coefficient involves (1) administering one form of a test, (2) splitting the test items into two equivalent halves (e.g., odd and even items), (3) scoring each half, (4) correlating scores on the two halves, and then (5) correcting this reliability estimate by the Spearman-Brown formula. The steps followed are presented in detail below.

1. Suppose on a 20-item test (from our previous example, Exhibit 5.1), odd- and even-numbered items are scored separately. Scores were as follows:

Student	Odds	Evens	Student	Odds	Evens
A	5	5	F	4	5
B	9	7	G	10	10
C	7	5	H	6	8
D	7	7	I	5	8
E	8	7	J	8	8
K	9	8	P	9	9
L	7	6	Q	6	8
M	6	5	R	7	8
N	9	7	S	5	7
O	6	8	T	8	7
U	6	9	Z	6	6
V	9	8	AA	6	8
W	6	5	BB	6	8
X	7	6	CC	4	6
Y	9	10	DD	6	5
EE	10	9	JJ	7	6
FF	6	6	KK	8	8
GG	8	7	LL	4	4
HH	6	7	MM	5	9
II	7	10	NN	8	10

2. The correlation between the two halves can be found using any of several formulas (see Appendix A), for example:

$$r_{oe} = \frac{n\Sigma X_o X_e - (\Sigma X_o)(\Sigma X_e)}{\sqrt{n\Sigma X_o^2 - (\Sigma X_o)^2}\,\sqrt{n\Sigma X_e^2 - (\Sigma X_e)^2}}$$

where X_o = score on the odd items, X_e = score on the even items, and n = the number of pairs of scores. Thus, our first task is to find $\Sigma X_o, \Sigma X_o^2, \Sigma X_e, \Sigma X_e^2$ and $\Sigma X_o X_e$.

EXHIBIT 5.2 (*Continued*)

$\Sigma X_o = 5 + 9 + 7 + \cdots + 5 + 8 = 275$
$\Sigma X_o^2 = (5)^2 + (9)^2 + (7)^2 + \cdots + (5)^2 + (8)^2 = 1,993$
$\Sigma X_e = 5 + 7 + 5 + \cdots + 9 + 10 = 290$
$\Sigma X_e^2 = (5)^2 + (7)^2 + (5)^2 + \cdots + (9)^2 + (10)^2 = 2,202$
$\Sigma X_o X_e = (5)(5) + (9)(7) + (7)(5) + \cdots + (5)(9) + (8)(10) = 2,046$

Substituting in the equation:

$$r_{oe} = \frac{40\,(2046) - (275)(290)}{\sqrt{40\,(1993) - (275)^2}\,\sqrt{40\,(2202) - (290)^2}} = .52$$

This value ($r_{oe} = .52$) is the correlation between scores on the odd and even items.

3. As this reliability estimate is based on two 10-item tests, and we want to estimate the reliability of the total test, which is 20 items long, we correct for length of the test by using the Spearman-Brown formula, which in this case is:

$$r_{tt} = \frac{2r_{oe}}{1 + r_{oe}} = (2)(.52)/1 + .52 = .68$$

This value ($r = .68$) is the estimated reliability of the 20-item test. While we would prefer a higher value, .68 is not inordinately low for a classroom test of only 20 items.

ITEM ANALYSIS

The analyses described in the preceding section considered performance on the test as a whole. But as each individual item was selected for inclusion on the test because it measured an important bit of knowledge and/or an important skill, it would also be useful to analyze and evaluate the individual items comprising the test. The generic term given to statistical analyses of item characteristics is *item analysis.*

Item analyses have two purposes. First, by identifying defective items they enable us to improve our tests and evaluation procedures. Second, and more important, by indicating which material students have and have not mastered, particularly what skills they lack and what material still causes difficulty, we can plan, revise, and improve our instruction. To illustrate, if item analysis of a test covering exponents showed that students had mastered the skills needed when manipulating exponents except for the use of negative exponents, the teacher could both review this material before proceeding to the next topic and also plan to teach the topic in a different manner in succeeding terms.

Typically, item analyses are used to study three characteristics of items: the difficulty of the item, the discrimination power of the item, and the effectiveness of the alternatives. For each analysis, there is a variety of procedures and statistics which can be used (see, e.g., Ebel, 1965; Davis, 1951; Wood, 1960), but our presentation will illustrate only simple methods of item analysis. We do this for several reasons. First, these simple methods clearly illustrate the basic procedures of item analysis and thus will give an understanding of the logic of the analyses. Second, there is no persuasive evidence that the complex procedures provide better or more usable information to the classroom teacher than do simpler methods. And, third, because of limited time and facilities, the classroom teacher, if he is to perform an item analysis, will usually find the simpler methods to be more feasible.

We should also note that item analysis procedures have been developed primarily for alternative-choice items. However, with minor procedural alterations they can be applied to other types of items. We will, however, confine our illustrations to alternative-choice items.

Discrimination

One measure of the effectiveness of an item would be its ability to discriminate between students who vary in their degree of knowledge of the material tested. If we had two groups of students, one of which was composed of students who had thoroughly mastered the material and the other of students who had not, we would expect a larger portion of the former group to correctly answer any test item. An *item discrimination index* provides a measure of the ability of an item to discriminate between the two groups.

The problem, of course, is how to define the groups that are to be compared. Although it would be preferable to use some criterion external to the test (e.g., performance in a subsequent course, ability to apply the knowledge to "real life" situations), such indices usually are not available. Thus we utilize a criterion internal to the test,[3] the usual measure being the total score on the test. That is, we assume that the total test is an adequate measure of

---

[3] If items are evaluated against a criterion external to the test, we are measuring item validity; when criteria internal to the test are used, we more properly speak of item discrimination indices.

students' ability and, consequently, that students who obtain higher total scores have a greater degree of mastery than those obtaining lower scores.

The next step is to select the groups to be contrasted. The prime requirement is to use large enough samples so that our statistics will be stable. While it can be shown that, with a normal distribution of scores, use of the highest and lowest scoring 27 percent of students is an optimal procedure, the difference between using this percentage of students and some other percentage (say, 25, 30, or 33 percent) will not be great. Furthermore, in the typical class, use of only the extreme 25 to 33 percent may result in very small groups for analyses. Thus the teacher may want to contrast the upper and lower halves of the class. This latter procedure will result in larger groups and, in addition, will provide a more stringent test of discrimination power, as it uses all data, not just extreme groups.

To recapitulate, the operational procedure for developing groups will be: (1) rank all test papers in order, from highest to lowest, on the basis of total score; (2) select the two subgroups ("high" and "low") by taking the necessary number of tests from each end.

The next step is to tally the frequency of each response to each item for each subgroup. Then convert these frequencies to proportions by dividing by the number of students in the subgroup. An example, using four items from an examination in a testing course, is presented in Figure 5.3; in this example, the class of 40 students was divided into an upper and lower half ($n = 20$ in each group).

The discrimination index may be defined as the proportion in the "high" group passing the item minus the proportion in the "low" group passing the item:

$$\text{Discrimination index} = P_{high} - P_{low} \qquad (5.4)$$

In other words, the discrimination index is the difference in the proportion of the high and low groups passing an item. The magnitude of the index indicates the degree and the sign indicates the direction of discrimination.

What is an acceptable level of discrimination? Obviously, as the index is defined, high positive values are preferable. Indices higher than .35–.40 denote good items; items with indices of .20 or higher discriminate somewhat but probably can be improved; indices near zero indicate weak items that do not discriminate; and items with negative indices discriminate in the wrong direction, that is, more of the poorer students obtain correct answers than do better students.

Applying these standards to the items in Figure 5.3, we find that item III provides good discrimination, item II discriminates positively but could be improved, item I does not discriminate at all, and item IV discriminates negatively.

The teacher who has access to automatic data processing equipment could calculate more complex item discrimination indices.

FIGURE 5.3

ILLUSTRATIVE ITEM ANALYSIS DATA

The following table gives the response pattern and item analysis data for four multiple-choice items ($N = 20$ in each group; * indicates correct response).

Item		Responses				Proportions			
		A	B	C*	D	A	B	C*	D
I	High	0	1	19	0	.00	.05	.95	.00
	Low	0	2	18	0	.00	.10	.90	.00
		Difficulty = .95 + .90/2 = .92				Discrimination = .95 − .90 = .05			
		A*	B	C	D	A*	B	C	D
II	High	16	2	0	2	.80	.10	.00	.10
	Low	12	4	0	4	.60	.20	.00	.20
		Difficulty = .80 + .60/2 = .70				Discrimination = .80 − .60 = .20			
		A	B	C*	D	A	B	C*	D
III	High	3	2	13	2	.15	.10	.65	.10
	Low	8	3	5	4	.40	.15	.25	.20
		Difficulty = .65 + .25/2 = .45				Discrimination = .65 − .25 = .40			
		A	B*	C	D	A	B*	C	D
IV	High	2	4	14	0	.10	.20	.70	.00
	Low	4	8	6	2	.20	.40	.30	.10
		Difficulty = .20 + .40/2 = .30				Discrimination = .20 − .40 = − .20			

The indices most frequently used are based on (1) the covariation of item and test scores and (2) the correlation between scores on an individual item and the total test score. These analyses indicate if the individual item is measuring the same thing as the total test.

Difficulty

The second dimension is item difficulty, which is usually defined as the percentage of students obtaining the correct answer to an item:

$$\text{Item difficulty} = \frac{P_{high} + P_{low}}{2} \qquad (5.5)$$

That is, it is the average difficulty of the item for the two groups. Item difficulty obviously could be measured in other ways; for example, we could directly tally the number of persons correctly answering each item.

What is an optimal difficulty level for items? It can be shown that to maximize discrimination among individuals, items of medium difficulty (i.e., difficulty $\sim .50$) are optimal and that very easy and very difficult items, in turn, do not provide much discrimination between persons. Therefore, when building standardized tests, test constructors usually strive for a distribution of items having a mean difficulty of .50–.60; they do, however, include some difficult items to provide discrimination at the upper end and some easy ones to provide discrimination at the lower end of the score distribution.

On a classroom exam, the teacher may use other levels of difficulty, depending upon the function of the item or test. For example, many tests start with a few easy (difficulty $\sim .90$) items as "warm-up" items. Or, a test used to check if an assignment had been read might include only items that would be very easy for people who had read the assignment.

The example (Figure 5.3) includes a very easy item (I), a relatively easy item (II), one of medium difficulty (III), and a very hard item (IV).

Effectiveness of Alternatives

Item difficulty and discrimination indices, while measuring important characteristics of items, do not indicate why the items operate as they do. By looking at the pattern of responses to alternatives, however, the teacher can often obtain clues as to how an item operated. These clues, in turn, may indicate how the test can be improved and/or where teaching and learning was ineffective.

The types of clues are several. We can look for alternatives that attract no responses; these alternatives obviously do not aid in discrimination. Or we can look for very popular alternatives. Or we can look for alternatives that attract certain types of students; for example, alternatives that appear to mislead only the better students.

To illustrate the value of item analyses, look at the individual items in Figure 5.3.

Item I is very easy, does not discriminate, and B is the only distractor drawing any responses. Although it might appear that changing alternatives A and D might strengthen the item, with an item this easy it is unlikely that the item will become more difficult, and thus possibly discriminate better, without a complete rewriting of the item.

Item II is relatively easy and discriminates in the right direction but not to as great a degree as would be desired. The obvious first step in revising this item is to strengthen alternative C.

Item III is slightly more difficult that the average item but discriminates well. All alternatives draw some responses but A is particularly attractive to the poorer students. Thus it probably indicates a common misconception or error by students who have not mastered the material covered by the item and should provide clues regarding needed instructional changes.

Item IV is difficult and discriminates negatively. Note particularly that alternative C is more attractive to the better students than the correct response. When this pattern of response occurs it usually indicates a defective item with more than one plausible response. (Of course, the item may simply be miskeyed.)

Must Items Discriminate?

Use of discrimination indices to evaluate items implies that items which discriminate between individuals are better items than those that do not discriminate. But do we always prefer tests which discriminate between individuals? As tests are typically used in the classroom, discrimination usually is an important concern. Certainly when tests are used to rank students—for example, as a basis for grading or course sectioning—the better the items discriminate between students, the more effective the test will be as a measure of relative achievement. Conversely, items that do not discriminate do not contribute to measurement.

But there are situations where discrimination is of lesser importance. If the testing goal is to assess students' level of mastery of important skills or content, then discrimination between students is of secondary importance. That is, we are primarily interested in describing each student's level of attainment, not in differentiating between students. We may wish to compare students' performance to a predetermined standard of mastery, but here again, discrimination between students would be relatively unimportant.

An example is the proposed National Assessment of Educational Progress (Tyler, Merwin, and Ebel, 1966). This study is designed to determine the extent to which American students have mastered certain educational skills and knowledge. Although comparisons will be made between various samples, the goal of the study is to describe typical performance, not discriminate between individual students. Thus items will be included on the assessment only if they represent important educational skills and outcomes.

Or consider another situation where discrimination power is irrelevant. Where mastery of a particular skill is necessary before a more complex skill (which builds on the prior skill) can be taught, we must be assured that students have mastered the prior skill (cf. Gagné, 1967). Suppose, for example, that we wanted to teach students how to balance chemical equations. To try to teach this skill to students who lacked an understanding of algebraic equations would be futile. Thus, before beginning instruction, we might want to measure their ability to manipulate algebraic formulae. On such a test, the ability of items to discriminate between individuals would be of little importance.

The classroom teacher, also, may properly include items on her tests which measure skills that she considers important and relevant, regardless of whether they discriminate between students. However, when doing so, she should be certain that the items are well constructed (according to other relevant standards of item quality) and are used in situations where discrimination ability is, in fact, irrelevant in light of the purposes of the testing.

A similar question can be raised regarding the appropriate difficulty of test items. We mentioned that items of medium difficulty generally provide the best discrimination but, for some purposes, easy or difficult items may be preferable. Here it is important to remember that the difficulty of an item will be a function of both the item and the group being tested. Thus an item may be answered correctly because students have mastered the material or because the phrasing of the item gives away the correct answer. Conversely, students may have mastered the material tested by an item, but the structure of the item may cause them to answer incorrectly. Furthermore, we cannot assume that answers reflect only what has been learned in the class; responses may be based on materials learned in other classes or outside the formal educational structure.

SUMMARY

This chapter continued the discussion of classroom tests begun in the previous chapter by considering the scoring and analysis of tests and of individual items.

Accurate scoring was seen as requiring three elements: (1) the student unambiguously recording his response, (2) a list of correct responses and permissible variations, the scoring key, and (3) a procedure for comparing students' responses to the scoring key. Problems in scoring various types of items were briefly considered.

The discussion of analyzing test scores focused on techniques for describing score distributions and on methods for determining the consistency and validity of classroom tests.

Three types of item analyses were illustrated: item discrimination indices, item difficulty indices, and analysis of the effectiveness of the alternatives.

Emphasis was on how item data are analyzed and what information each analysis provides, both for improving tests and for improving instruction.

REFERENCES

DAVIS, F. B. "Item Selection Techniques," in E. F. LINDQUIST (ed.), *Educational Measurement,* chap. 9. Washington, D.C.: American Council on Education, 1951.

DAVIS, F. B. *Educational Measurements and Their Interpretation.* Belmont, Calif.: Wadsworth Publishing Co., Inc., 1964.

EBEL, R. L. *Measuring Educational Achievement.* Englewood Cliffs, N.J.: Prentice-Hall, Inc., 1965.

EDWARDS, A. L. *Statistical Analysis.* 3rd ed. New York: Holt, Rinehart & Winston, Inc., 1969.

GAGNÉ, R. M. "Instructional Variables and Learning Outcomes." (Paper presented at the Symposium on Problems in the Evaluation of Instruction, University of California, Los Angeles, 1967.)

TYLER, R. W.; MERWIN, J. C., and EBEL, R. L. "Symposium: A National Assessment of Educational Progress," *Journal of Educational Measurement*, Vol. 3 (1966), pp. 1–17.

WOOD, D. A. *Test Construction.* Columbus, Ohio: Charles E. Merrill Publishing Co., 1960.

6

STANDARDIZED ACHIEVEMENT TESTS

Teacher-made classroom tests play a large and necessary role in the educational process. Certainly no other assessment technique permits as good an evaluation of the extent to which local educational goals have been attained as does the well-constructed classroom test. Yet situations are frequently encountered where an *ad hoc* teacher-made test will not suffice—e.g., when comparing achievement in several areas, when measuring educational growth over a period of years, when comparing students to norm groups broader than the local school. In all of these situations, standardized measures will provide more accurate measurement.

Standardized achievement tests differ from teacher-made tests in several ways. As they are designed for use in a variety of schools, they will cover material that is widely accepted by subject matter experts as being basic to the field, not just the material that one teacher deems vital. As they will be administered to diverse groups of students, the range of item difficulty will be broader than on classroom tests. Item format will generally be limited to alternative-choice, usually multiple-choice, items. The test publisher, when constructing the test, will subject items to intensive pretesting, tryout, and item analysis procedures. Norms will be developed for various groups of students, defined by several dimensions—e.g., geographic region, time of year, grade level, type of school, sex. Except for tests designed for elementary grades, items will be printed in reusable booklets, and students will respond on separate machine-scorable answer sheets.

In short, when developing standardized tests, test publishers attempt to accurately measure widely taught basic skills and to provide means for interpreting scores with reference to broad-scale, but clearly defined, norm groups. (See ETS, 1965, or Chauncey and Dobbin, 1963, for a more detailed description of the procedures followed.)

MEASURING ACHIEVEMENT

One's first inclination might be to define *achievement tests* as those tests that measure what the student has learned. However, a little reflection will indicate that all tests measure what the student has learned—what his developed skills and abilities are. The label "achievement test," therefore, is generally applied to tests that measure the results of learning which has occurred as a result of relatively formal and structured educational experiences. The content area covered may be narrow, as in a classroom test, or quite broad, as knowledge of a foreign language or ability to do arithmetic reasoning. Furthermore, an achievement test focuses on the past or present—what the student has learned or what he knows or can do. In constructing an achievement test, the *sine qua non* is representative sampling of the relevant domain; that is, content validity is the preeminent concern.

We have already discussed (in Chapters 1 and 4) many of the possible uses of achievement tests. But to recapitulate, standardized achievement tests are particularly useful when comparing students or making generalizations that extend beyond the individual classroom. Thus they are used to measure students' academic growth from year to year, to measure skills resulting from learning experiences broader than the teachings of a particular class, to compare an individual's relative performance in several domains, and to compare students to wider scale norm groups (e.g., regional or national samples). They are also used for selecting students for special programs, for placing students in various "tracks" or course sequences, and for the evaluation of instructional methods and materials.

Although in some circumstances achievement tests may be administered several times a year (for example, when measuring reading skills in the primary grades), the more typical pattern is for achievement batteries to be administered only once each year or even every other year. Testing will probably be more frequent during the elementary school years, where development is rapid and the curriculum concentrates on a small number of fundamental skills.

Assumptions

When measuring achievement using standardized tests we make several assumptions. First, we assume that the important educational outcomes can be specified. These outcomes guide the test construction process, for unless we can specify exactly what outcomes we wish to measure, we cannot plan and develop an instrument to measure these outcomes. Two aspects of this specification are particularly important. As a standardized test is developed for use in a wide variety of schools, the abilities tested will be ones that are quite widely accepted; thus the test content may not reflect the educational goals of an individual teacher or school system. And, although achievement tests focus on the past (what the student has learned) and the present (his present level of achievement), they also have a future reference. That is, what are considered important goals are usually skills which will transfer to a number of future learning situations, both within and without the classroom.

Second, we assume that the tests we build accurately assess these important outcomes. By "accurately" we refer both to consistency and validity. The need for consistent (reliable) measurement has been explained previously, as has the fact that, with achievement tests, evidence of content validity is the predominant concern. It is in the latter case that the problem of differing goals becomes an operational question.

Third, we assume that meaningful norms and standards are available to aid in interpretation of scores. Although, in most educational situations, content (criterion-referenced) scores would be desirable, in practice such scores generally are not available. Thus interpretations will generally be norm-referenced and a student's score will be compared to other students who are, in some important ways, similar to him. Operationally, this means that diverse and extensive normative data must be provided.

Finally, if an individual's scores are to be meaningful, he must have had the opportunity to learn the skills and content covered by the test. Moreover, for scores of two (or more) individuals to be completely comparable, they must have had approximately equal exposure to the material, or at least equal opportunities to learn. In measuring the attainment of the goals of a fairly circumscribed program, such as in the typical classroom examination, this is little problem, as students will have been through the same educational experiences. When testing broader skills or diverse groups the problem becomes more crucial, as students' opportunities to learn may vary widely.

Students from lower socioeconomic levels and members of minority groups provide a clear and important illustration. These students often have not had the educational opportunities, either within school or outside school, that some of their more fortunate age-mates have had. Consequently, they frequently obtain lower test scores. However, these scores may reflect their background and educational opportunities more than they reflect the students' abilities. The lesson is clear—test scores can never be interpreted in isolation; one must always consider the educational opportunities the student has had.

Types of Standardized Achievement Tests

There are three classes of standardized achievement tests: survey tests, diagnostic tests, and readiness tests.

SURVEY TESTS. Survey tests, as the name implies, are designed to broadly sample knowledge and skills in a field; that is, they survey what students can do and what they know. The area covered by a survey test usually is quite broadly defined—e.g., English literature, arithmetic reasoning, spelling, reading comprehension. Regardless of the content area covered, the function of a survey test is to provide an estimate of the student's mastery of the field. Thus usually only one summary (total) score is computed.

Although a survey test may stand alone, more commonly it is part of a test battery. A *test battery* is a series of tests administered jointly, each one covering a different domain, with scores based on a common norm group. An achievement test battery may contain from several to a dozen or more separate tests, depending on the breadth of the battery and the coverage of each individual test. Several levels of the test are usually constructed, each appropriate for several adjacent grades, thus providing an integrated series of tests that can be used over a wide age range. In addition, equivalent forms of the tests are usually provided at each age level.

To illustrate, the Comprehensive Tests of Basic Skills are published in four overlapping[1] levels—grades 2.5–4, 4–6, 6–8 and 8–12. At each level, four areas are tested—reading, language, arithmetic and study skills—and within each area several subsidiary skills are measured (for example, the arithmetic area includes computations, concepts, and applications). Brief descriptions of a number of standardized achievement batteries can be found in Appendix B. A more detailed description of a typical standardized achievement battery is presented in Exhibit 6.1.

EXHIBIT 6.1
DESCRIPTION OF A STANDARDIZED ACHIEVEMENT TEST BATTERY
Stanford Achievement Test Series

Publisher: Harcourt Brace Jovanovich Test Department

Purpose: To measure current instructional goals, both content and skills, in basic curricular areas; attempts to attain a balance between traditional educational goals and newer curricular trends; provides continuous assessment from prekindergarten through grade 12.

Levels: There are five levels of the Elementary level battery:

Primary I, grades 1.5–2.4 Primary II, grades 2.5–3.9

Intermediate I, grades 4.0–5.4 Intermediate II, grades 5.5–6.9

Advanced, grades 7.0–9.9

In addition there is a High School level battery for grades 9–12.

Forms: There are three equivalent forms at each level of the Elementary battery and two equivalent forms of the High School battery. Tests may be either hand or machine scored; publisher provides a machine-scoring service which includes summary reports.

Scores and norms: On Elementary levels scores are reported in grade scores and grade equivalents, stanines, and percentile ranks. High School battery reports percentile ranks and stanines, by grades, for both total and college preparatory groups. Individual profile charts, cumulative record forms, and interpretive manuals are available.

---

[1] Overlapping levels, besides providing continuity, add flexibility. For example, suppose a test has one level for grades 2–4 and another for grades 4–6. In a high-achieving fourth-grade class we would use the higher level, while in a class making slower progress we would use the lower level.

EXHIBIT 6.1 (*Continued*)

Content: The coverage of the various levels is briefly described below. (See Figure 6.1 for examples of items.)

Primary I. Word Reading—matching word symbols with pictures; Paragraph Meaning—comprehension of meaning of two or more sentences; Vocabulary—dictation test of definitions, synonyms, associations; Spelling; Word Study Skills—auditory recognition of beginning and ending sounds; Arithmetic—measures, problem solving, number concepts. i/t/a edition available. 3 hours.

Primary II. Word Meaning—vocabulary in reading context; Paragraph Meaning: Science and Social Studies Concepts—vocabulary in these areas measured independent of reading skill; Spelling; Word Study Skills—recognition of phonic generalizations; Language—capitalization, punctuation, correct usage; Arithmetic Computation—skill in fundamental operations; Arithmetic Concepts—concepts of numbers and measures, problem solving. 4 hours.

Intermediate I. Word Meaning; Paragraph Meaning; Spelling: Word Study Skills; Language; Arithmetic Computation; Arithmetic Concepts; Arithmetic Applications; Social Studies; Science. 5 hours.

Intermediate II. Same as Intermediate I but deletes Word Study Skills. 5 hours.

Advanced. Same as Intermediate II but deletes Word Meaning. 5 hours.

High School. English; Numerical Competence; Mathematics; Reading; Science; Social Studies; Spelling. Supplemental tests available for Arts and Humanities; Business and Economics; Technical Comprehension—industrial arts and applied science. 5½ hours.

For Intermediate I and higher levels, partial batteries (generally eliminating Science and Social Studies tests) are available.

Supplemental Tests: A number of other tests are available from the publisher which supplement the basic battery described above. These include:

Stanford Early School Achievement Test. Two levels, K–1.1, 1.2–1.6; will include tests of The Environment—meaning of words in social studies and science; Mathematics—concepts of counting, measurement, conservation of number, space, and volume; Letters and Sounds—upper and lower case letters, beginning sounds; Aural Comprehension; designed to measure what children have learned rather than readiness or potential. 1½ hours.

Diagnostic Tests in Reading and Arithmetic. Designed to measure

EXHIBIT 6.1 (Concluded)
specific strengths and weaknesses in these fundamental areas. Reading Level I (2.5–4.5) measures Reading Comprehension, Vocabulary, Auditory Discrimination, Syllabication, Beginning and Ending Sounds, Blending, Sound Discrimination; Level II (4.5–8.5) measures Reading Comprehension, Vocabulary, Syllabication, Sound Discrimination, Blending, Rate of Reading. Arithmetic Level I measures Concepts of Numbers and Numerals, Computation and Number Facts; Level II measures Concepts of Numbers and Numerals, Computations with Whole Numbers, Common Fractions, Decimal Fractions, Percent and Number Facts.

Modern Mathematics Concepts Test. Can be used as supplement to, or in place of, arithmetic concepts tests; two levels— Intermediate II (5–6) and Advanced (7–9).

Evaluation: One of the most widely used achievement batteries; meticulously constructed and standardized. (For a more detailed evaluation see Mehrens and Lehmann, 1969, pp. 170–86.)

Some batteries place primary emphasis on sampling content domains; that is, they identify major content areas, then develop tests to sample these content domains. Other batteries emphasize skills and abilities which underlie performance in a number of areas and transfer to various tasks. These batteries stress language skills, mathematical reasoning, ability to interpret reading materials, study skills (interpreting graphs and tables, dictionary skills, etc.), and similar skills. Individual items may test diverse skills, from recall of factual material, through applications of principles to new situations, to the evaluation and analysis of data. (Some examples of items from survey achievement batteries are shown in Figure 6.1.)

Survey tests which are not a part of a battery generally are one of two types. Some measure fundamental skills that merit frequent and repeated testing—for example, the measurement of reading skills in the primary grades. Others are designed to measure achievement in quite specific content areas. An example would be the College Level Examination Program (sponsored by the College Entrance Examination Board), which includes tests in Introductory Calculus, General Chemistry, American Government, and similar areas. As one use of these tests is to grant advanced placement or credit for independent study, the tests, in one sense, are standardized end-of-course examinations.

FIGURE 6.1

EXAMPLES OF ITEMS ON SURVEY ACHIEVEMENT TESTS: STANFORD ACHIEVEMENT TEST, INTERMEDIATE I

TEST 1:   Word Meaning

DIRECTIONS: Read the beginning part of each sentence and the words under it. Decide which of the answers given is *best.* Look at the answer spaces at the right or on your answer sheet (if you have one). Fill in the space which has the same number as the word you have chosen.

SAMPLES

A The name of a color is —

1 farm	3 red	
2 milk	4 pet	

    1 2 3 4
A ◯ ◯ ◍ ◯

B The day that comes after Monday is —

5 Sunday	7 Wednesday
6 Tuesday	8 Saturday

    5 6 7 8
B ◯ ◯ ◯ ◯

TEST 2:   Paragraph Meaning

DIRECTIONS: Read each paragraph below. Decide which of the numbered words or phrases below the paragraph is *best* for each blank. Look at the answer spaces at the right or on your answer sheet (if you have one). Fill in the space which has the same number as the word(s) you have chosen.

SAMPLES

The singing birds entertain us. We like to A their B.

A	1 touch	3 hear
	2 see	4 feel

    1 2 3 4
A ◯ ◯ ◍ ◯

B	5 songs	7 flight
	6 colors	8 tricks

    5 6 7 8
B ◯ ◯ ◯ ◯

TEST 3: Spelling

DIRECTIONS: Read each of the groups of words below. One of the words in each group is misspelled. Find the word that has been misspelled. Look at the answer spaces at the right or on your answer sheet (if you have one). Fill in the space which has the same number as the word you have chosen.

SAMPLES

A   1 dog   3 walk   1   2   3   4
     2 boy   4 yse   A   ○   ○   ○   ◑

B   5 this   7 cold   5   6   7   8
     6 kap   8 tell   B   ○   ○   ○   ○

TEST 4: Word Study Skills   *Part A: Phonics*

DIRECTIONS: Read each word with a line under it, then read the three words just below it. The sound with a line under it in the first word is like a sound in one of the other three words. Say the first word to yourself and listen for the sound of the underlined letter (or letters). Then say the three words just below it and listen for the sound of the letter (or letters) underlined in the first word. When you find the word that has the same sound, look at the number beside the word. Then look at the answer spaces at the right or on your answer sheet (if you have one). Fill in the space which has the same number as the word you have chosen.

SAMPLES

A ride
      1 sick   2 fine   3 wish   1   2   3
                                                   A   ○   ◑   ○

B do
      4 go   5 no   6 to   4   5   6
                                                   B   ○   ○   ○

TEST 4: Word Study Skills (Continued)   *Part B: Syllabication*

DIRECTIONS: In each of the groups below are five words. Look at the first words in the group. Find the word beneath it which is divided the right way. Look at the answer spaces at the right or on your answer sheet (if you have one). Fill in the space which has the same number as the word you have chosen.

SAMPLES

C kitten
1 ki tten   3 kit ten   1   2   3   4
2 ki tt en   4 kitten   C   ○   ○   ◑   ○

D tomorrow
5 tom or row   7 tom o rrow   5   6   7   8
6 tomo rrow   8 to mor row   D   ○   ○   ○   ○

TEST 5: Language   *Part A: Usage*

DIRECTIONS: Read each sentence below. Decide which, *if either,* of the two choices in each sentence is correct in *standard written English.* Look at the answer spaces at the right or on your answer sheet (if you have one). If the choice numbered 1 is correct, fill in the space under the 1. If the choice numbered 2 is correct, fill in the space under 2. If neither choice 1 nor choice 2 is correct, fill in the space under N. ("N" stands for "neither.")

SAMPLES

A Joe $\frac{1 \text{ set}}{2 \text{ sat}}$ in the chair. .... A 1 2 N ○ ◉ ○

B Sally $\frac{1 \text{ ain't}}{2 \text{ aren't}}$ here. .... B 1 2 N ○ ○ ○

TEST 6: Arithmetic Computation

DIRECTIONS: Work the example in each box. Then look at the possible answers at the right side of the box and see if your answer is given. If it is, fill in the space at the right or on your answer sheet (if you have one) which has the same letter as the answer you have chosen. If your answer is *not* given, fill in the space which has the same letter as the letter beside the NG (which means "not given"). Use a separate sheet of paper for figuring.

SAMPLE A

64	a 31	a b c d e
−23	b 40	A ○ ○ ◉ ○ ○
41	c 41	
	d 42	
	e NG	

TEST 7: Arithmetic Concepts

DIRECTIONS: Read each question. Decide which of the answers given below is correct. Look at the answer spaces at the right or on your answer sheet (if you have one). Fill in the space which has the same letter as the answer you have chosen.

SAMPLE

A A dime is worth how many cents?

| a 2 | c 10 | a b c d |
| b 5 | d 25 | A ○ ○ ◉ ○ |

TEST 10:   Science

DIRECTIONS: Read each question. Decide which of the answers given below is *best*. Look at the answer spaces at the right or on your answer sheet (if you have one). Fill in the space which has the same number as the answer you have chosen.

SAMPLE

A As water boils, it changes to ___

1 ice	3 steam
2 dew	4 snow

1 2 3 4
A ○ ○ ◉ ○

Note: The items reproduced above are practice items used only to illustrate the format of the items and responding procedures. The actual test items are more complex and difficult; for example a series of items may be based on one reading passage or a particular graph.

Source: Items reprinted with permission of Harcourt Brace Jovanovich, Inc., © 1965.

DIAGNOSTIC TESTS.   A different type of test is needed when working with students who are having difficulty mastering some aspect of the curriculum. Often their trouble appears to be caused by some specific aspect of the learning situation. If we could pinpoint the source of their difficulty, we could provide appropriate remedial help and thereby facilitate future learning. Diagnostic tests are designed for this purpose.

The development of a diagnostic test starts with the identification of the component elements making up a skill; then groups of items (subtests) are developed to measure each component. For example, a diagnostic reading test might include subtests measuring rate of reading, comprehension level, vocabulary, word analysis skills, and so forth. After a diagnostic test is administered, we identify the student's strengths and weaknesses (i.e., his pattern of high and low scores on the various subtests), determine which facets are causing the most difficulty, and institute remedial help to correct his deficiencies.

As might be expected, diagnostic tests are most common in reading and mathematics, skills that transfer to many different course areas.

READINESS TESTS.   A third type of achievement test is the readiness test. Again, the function of the test is indicated by its name: Does the student possess the prerequisite skills to profit from instruction in an area? For example, reading readiness tests, probably the most common type of readiness measure, are designed to ascertain if students have the necessary abilities (e.g., vocabulary, letter recognition or discrimination, ability to follow directions) to profit from beginning reading instruction. Although readiness tests are achievement tests, because they measure level of mastery of certain skills, they also function as aptitude tests because they predict future performance.

INTERPRETING SCORES ON ACHIEVEMENT TESTS

Although the classroom teacher will probably not be involved in the construction or statistical analysis of standardized tests, she is likely to have frequent need to interpret scores on standardized achievement tests. The interpretation may be only to aid her understanding of a student, or she may have to interpret scores to the student, parents, or other persons concerned with the student's education. We will next discuss the interpretation of standardized achievement tests.

What Does the Test Measure?

When interpreting scores on an achievement test—or on any test, for that matter—the first question one must ask is: What does the test measure? In measuring achievement, we are asking what content is covered by the test and what skills are required to successfully answer the test items.

In essence, we are trying to determine the content validity of the test. This, you will recall, is best accomplished by a thorough and systematic study of the items comprising the test. Valuable information can also be obtained by reading the description of the item sampling and test construction procedures in the test manual and from studies and reviews of the test.

Remember, also, that any achievement test is designed to sample a particular content, skill, or content/skill domain defined by the test constructors. And, as we have so often emphasized, the test constructor's definition may not coincide with the one preferred by the test user. Thus the teacher must ask yet another question: Does this test measure what I want to measure? If the answer is "no," the test is inappropriate for his purposes and should not be used.

We should also ask a corollary question: How accurately does the test measure whatever it measures? This, of course, is the reliability question. Although, by and large, standardized achievement tests are highly reliable ($r_{tt} > .90$ on many tests), all test scores are subject to some measurement error and cannot be interpreted with absolute precision. Thus, when interpreting individual scores, particularly when comparing a student's performance in several areas on the same battery (e.g., his score on the mathematics section with his score on the reading section) or his growth from year to year, we must always take unreliability of measurement into account. The danger is the tendency to consider relatively small differences in scores as representing true differences in achievement when, in fact, they may only reflect measurement errors.

Interindividual Comparisons

Scores on achievement tests, particularly survey tests, are usually interpreted in norm-referenced terms; that is, an individual student's performance is interpreted by comparing it to a relevant norm group. The critical consideration is, of course, the composition of the norm group used. As we have already discussed norm groups in some detail (in Chapter 3) we will not repeat the discussion here. We would only mention that, in education, the most appropriate norm group will usually be one composed of students who are in the same grade, from the same type of school and community, and who have had educational experiences comparable to the person whose score is being interpreted. If none of the normative data provided by the test publisher meet these and any other relevant requirements, the test user may have to develop local norms.

Any of several types of scores may be used to describe performance, with percentile ranks, standard scores, and grade scores being most frequently used. Although grade scores may seem most appropriate, they may be misleading unless students truly have had comparable educational experiences. To describe Sam Smith's arithmetic achievement by a grade score of 4–6 makes sense only if he has taken the same sequence of courses as has the typical fourth-grade student. Otherwise we may infer that he has mastered an area where, in fact, he has no experience.[2]

Because of problems with grade scores, many persons prefer to use *percentiles within grades*—that is, to express the student's score as a percentile ranking within a norm group composed solely

---

[2] See the discussion of grade scores in Chapter 3.

of his grade-mates. To further refine the norm group, some people advocate using *modal age grade norms*, norm groups composed of students whose grade placement is normal for their age and eliminating all persons whose progress has been accelerated or retarded.

Intraindividual Comparisons

Many test interpretations are based on intraindividual comparisons. One obvious example is comparing a student's relative performance on the various tests in an achievement battery. Suppose that the Iowa Tests of Basic Skills are administered in a school. By studying a student's profile of scores (see Figure 6.2) we can identify his relative strengths and weaknesses, the areas where he is achieving satisfactorily and the areas where he is having difficulty, and thus better plan his educational experiences. On this battery, we can also compare subtests within areas (e.g., the various language or arithmetic skills) to obtain even more detailed interpretations of his achievement.[3]

As learning is cumulative, usually we are also interested in the student's educational development from year to year. Since, on achievement batteries, each level is applicable to several grades, we can compare students' performance on the same test over a period of several years (see Figure 6.2). Furthermore, achievement series usually contain several levels. Although the same areas may not be tested at each level, because different skills are emphasized at different grade levels, there is integration between levels, thus permitting growth over longer periods of time to be studied.

Another frequently used comparison is between students' achievement and an estimate of their academic ability or intelligence. This comparison assumes that a student's achievement should be commensurate with his ability. (If achievement is below expectations, the student may be labeled an "underachiever," and if his achievement surpasses his ability level he may be tabbed an "overachiever.") As was pointed out earlier, such interpretations are best avoided, both because of the statistical problems in comparing scores and because of the assumption that intelligence is the sole determiner of achievement.

Finally, we should mention that a student's achievement, as

---

[3] Intraindividual comparisons have a normative base, as the interpretation procedure is to first obtain normative scores for each scale, then compare these scores (within an individual).

FIGURE 6.2

AN EXAMPLE OF A PROFILE FROM A STANDARDIZED ACHIEVEMENT BATTERY: IOWA TESTS OF BASIC SKILLS

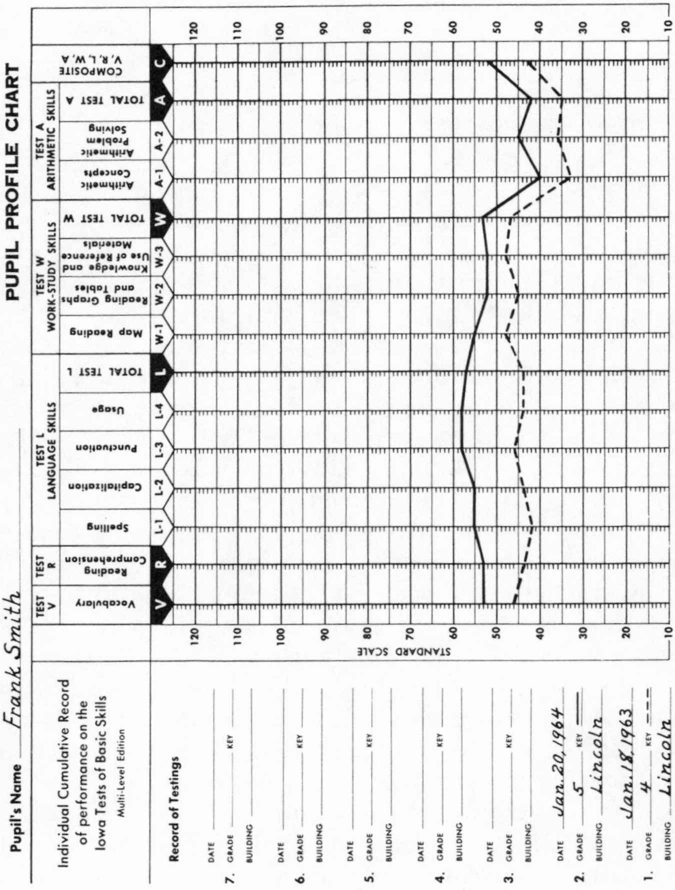

Pupil's Name _Frank Smith_

PUPIL PROFILE CHART

Individual Cumulative Record
of performance on the
Iowa Tests of Basic Skills
Multi-Level Edition

Record of Testings

7. DATE _____ KEY _____
   GRADE _____ BUILDING _____

6. DATE _____ KEY _____
   GRADE _____ BUILDING _____

5. DATE _____ KEY _____
   GRADE _____ BUILDING _____

4. DATE _____ KEY _____
   GRADE _____ BUILDING _____

3. DATE _____ KEY _____
   GRADE _____ BUILDING _____

2. DATE _Jan. 20, 1964_ KEY _____
   GRADE _5_ BUILDING _Lincoln_

1. DATE _Jan. 18, 1963_ KEY _____
   GRADE _4_ BUILDING _Lincoln_

measured by standardized tests, can be compared to his achievement measured in other ways—e.g., by classroom tests or teachers' judgments—or expressed through other types of performance—e.g., written assignments or class discussions. Although these various performances may require somewhat different abilities and skills and thus will not be in complete agreement with each other, large discrepancies will probably provide important clues for understanding students' educational development.

ISSUES IN ACHIEVEMENT TESTING

Standardized achievement tests, by and large, are among the best tests in the psychologist's arsenal. That is not to say that all published achievement tests are acceptable instruments—far from it. But there are a number of carefully constructed achievement tests on the market, ones that measure a variety of abilities with high degrees of reliability and which have normative data available from diverse and well-defined norm groups. Thus the educator who is selecting an achievement test, particularly if he is looking for a survey battery covering "basic" educational skills, usually will have a choice between several possibilities.[4]

Nevertheless, opinion is divided on a number of issues surrounding the use of achievement tests. We have already mentioned one of these several times—whether score interpretations should be primarily norm-referenced or criterion-referenced—and, as we will mention this issue again when discussing grading (Chapter 8), we will not consider it here. Rather, we will briefly discuss three other issues: (1) the implications of using alternative-choice items, (2) the relationship between testing and the curriculum, and (3) the use of achievement tests for placing students within the curriculum.

Reliance on Alternative-Choice Items

Standardized achievement tests are composed almost exclusively of "objective" items, primarily multiple-choice items. The reasons are several and obvious: the need for rapid and objective scoring procedures, broader content sampling, adaptability to a variety of content areas, and higher reliability and validity.

Yet a number of persons have criticized what they consider to be excessive reliance on a single item type. Hoffman (1961, 1962), for

---

[4] For a discussion of choosing an achievement test see Engelhart, 1964; ETS, 1961, or Brown, 1970, Chapter 9.

example, attacked multiple-choice questions on several counts.[5] For one, he argued that multiple-choice items are made more difficult by increasing their ambiguity, thus producing unfair questions. He also felt that items geared to the "average" student penalize students having great depth of knowledge, for these students will often spot weaknesses in the keyed (correct) response and consequently select incorrect alternatives. Furthermore, he criticized multiple-choice items for stressing factual recall and not testing certain skills that are important in academic endeavors—e.g., creativity, ability to marshall and support an argument. What sort of item he would substitute is not clearly specified but, presumably, it would be an open-ended variety like an essay or a problem.

Proponents of objective test items have rebutted Hoffman's arguments and pointed out the advantages of multiple-choice items (see, e.g., ETS, 1963; Chauncey and Dobbin, 1963). They point out that sophisticated forms of multiple-choice items can be (and have been) developed, items which measure, for example, the ability to evaluate and analyze material; that students must be able to identify currently accepted knowledge; that adequate content sampling and reliable measurement is possible only by use of objective questions; and that these tests have proven to be useful in a variety of educational situations. Even their proponents would, of course, admit that alternative-choice items do not measure all important skills; but, then no assessment technique does.

Several further points should be noted. Any assessment technique will sacrifice some desirable features in favor of others. The use of alternative-choice items promotes wide content sampling, objective scoring, and administrative feasibility at the expense of a possible loss in depth of response and failure to provide an opportunity for individual expression. A closely related point: Any testing method cannot be evaluated in isolation; it must be compared to other available methods. Thus even an imperfect measure, which surely tests are, may be the best available method. Furthermore, there may be undesirable consequences of not testing, as well as undesirable results from testing. (See, e.g., Ebel, 1964, or Hawes, 1964, for a discussion of the benefits of testing.) Finally, we return to the question of goals. Hoffman and other critics (e.g., Black, 1963) are really criticizing the outcomes valued by the

---

[5] Although Hoffman directed his attack primarily at college admissions tests, his criticisms apply to all alternative-choice items.

educational establishment because tests are designed to measure goals that educators have set, not to set the goals.

Tests and the Curriculum

This last point leads us directly to the next issue, the relationship between tests and the curriculum. This issue is expressed in various ways: for example, tests are said to determine the curriculum, teachers are accused of teaching to tests, and norms are often confused with standards.

Do tests determine the curriculum? Do teachers teach to tests? There is no doubt that some teachers give students concentrated practice on the types of items that will appear on standardized tests and/or teach them techniques to outwit the test. If the purpose of such preparation is to attempt to raise scores to make the students, the teacher, or the school look good, then we should question the practice.

But the situation is not always so clear. Suppose that an elementary school arithmetic curriculum stresses understanding concepts and deemphasizes computational skills, but the achievement battery used in the school contains two arithmetic tests, one stressing concepts and the other computational skills. The students generally score high on the former and lower on the latter. Miss Smith, the third-grade teacher, in anticipation of the test administration, schedules additional arithmetic drills. Is she teaching to the test? Is she letting the test determine the curriculum? Perhaps. However, we could argue that, although she is not following the local curricular emphases, she is stressing skills that many educators feel important (remember, the content of achievement batteries is determined by subject-matter experts). Consequently, increasing students' skills in this area, even if done in preparation for a specific test battery, might be seen as a desirable outcome. The crucial point is whether the skills taught are important and will transfer to other areas or only serve to increase test scores, whether we increase performance in the domain which the test items sample or just teach test-taking skills.

Another concern is the confusion between norms and standards. One frequently reads in a newspaper or hears reported at a PTA meeting that the average student at Westside Elementary School scored at, say, the 85th percentile on the national norms on the yearly achievement battery. The implication is that the educational program of the school is responsible for this level of performance and that achievement was higher than might be expected. Such conclusions are gratuitous. It may be that the school is located in a community where parents value education and where there are a variety of out-of-school educational opportunities, and, therefore, students might have achieved at this level regardless of the educational program of the school. Conversely, even below average achievement might reflect a tremendous teaching job in a culturally deprived area. Thus setting local standards in terms of national averages is too simplistic a solution. Neglecting comparative performance, one must also remember that the important concern is the degree to which the school system has accomplished its own goals, not the goals as defined by the test or national norms.

Evaluating Students

As grading is most properly based on classroom tests (see Chapter 8), the use of standardized achievement tests for evaluating students becomes most controversial when test scores are used to place students in various sections of classes or various curricular tracks. Here two questions are preeminent. First, do the advantages of sectioning and grouping outweigh the disadvantages? This question is the central one and can only be decided by empirical evidence and value judgments regarding the relative importance of various outcomes. The second question is more directly relevant to testing: If differential placement is to be used, what assessment techniques will be used to determine each individual's placement? As past performance is usually the best predictor of future performance, and as achievement tests measure past performance, they should play a major role in the placement decision. Their relative importance, in comparison to other predictors —e.g., academic aptitude, teacher's judgments—should be determined by empirical studies.

SUMMARY

Standardized achievement tests are constructed, usually by test publishing firms, to measure a number of important educational skills. As they are designed for use in a wide variety of settings, they measure commonly accepted goals, are paper-and-pencil tests, and rely primarily on alternative-choice items. Their major uses are to compare students' achievement in different fields, when making generalizations that extend beyond a single classroom, and for administrative purposes such as placing students within curricula.

There are three types of standardized achievement tests. Survey tests measure the mastery of a particular area and are usually part of a battery covering several content or skill areas. Diagnostic tests measure the important components of basic skills, such as reading, and identify strengths and weaknesses, thus aiding in planning remedial work. Readiness measures indicate if the student has the prerequisite skills to begin formal work in an area.

Score interpretations are usually normatively based; however, some of the most important comparisons are intraindividual, as when comparing a student's relative performance in various areas and measuring his educational growth from year to year.

Although achievement tests have been criticized on a number of counts—e.g., for relying on alternative-choice items, for directing the curriculum—by and large, standardized achievement tests attain higher levels of technical adequacy than does any other class of test.

REFERENCES

BLACK, H. *They Shall Not Pass.* New York: William Morrow & Co., Inc., 1963.

BROWN, F. G. *Principles of Educational and Psychological Testing.* Hinsdale, Ill.: The Dryden Press, 1970.

CHAUNCEY, H., and DOBBIN, J. E. *Testing: Its Place in Education Today.* New York: Harper & Row, Publishers, 1963.

EBEL, R. L. "The Social Consequences of Educational Testing," in *Proceedings of the 1963 Invitational Conference on Testing Problems,* pp. 130–43. Princeton, N.J.: Educational Testing Service, 1964.

EDUCATIONAL TESTING SERVICE. *Selecting an Achievement Test: Principles and Procedures.* (Evaluation and Advisory Service Series No. 3.) Princeton, N.J., 1961.

EDUCATIONAL TESTING SERVICE. *Multiple-Choice Questions: A Close Look.* Princeton, N.J., 1963.

EDUCATIONAL TESTING SERVICE. *ETS Builds a Test*. Princeton, N.J., 1965.

ENGELHART, M. D. "What to Look for in a Review of an Achievement Test," *Personnel and Guidance Journal*, Vol. 42 (1964), pp. 616–19.

HAWES, G. R. *Educational Testing for the Millions*. New York: McGraw-Hill Book Co., 1964.

HOFFMAN, B. "The Tyranny of Multiple-Choice Tests," *Harper's Magazine*, March, 1961, pp. 37–44.

HOFFMAN, B. *The Tyranny of Testing*. New York: Crowell Collier and Macmillan, Inc., 1962.

MEHRENS, W. A., and LEHMANN, I. J. *Standardized Tests in Education*. New York: Holt, Rinehart & Winston, Inc., 1969.

7

OTHER STANDARDIZED TESTS

The three previous chapters focused on achievement tests, tests which measure academic knowledge and skills. We now turn to two types of tests, aptitude tests and personality measures, that measure characteristics of students which are not so closely tied to specific content areas. The role of these tests in education is to increase our understanding of the student as a learner by providing information on characteristics that may influence his approach to learning tasks—his academic aptitude, special skills and talents, personality traits, habits, values, and interests.

MEASURES OF INTELLECTUAL ABILITY

After achievement tests, the most widely used educational tests are measures of intellectual ability or aptitude. Although achievement and aptitude tests share many features in common (for example, both are tests of maximal performance, both measure what students have learned, their item content and format are quite similar) they can be differentiated along several dimensions. Aptitude tests have a future reference, predicting what a student can learn, while achievement tests stress what has been learned. Second, aptitude tests usually measure characteristics that will transfer to a variety of situations; thus, they stress learning skills rather than mastery of specific content. And, third, the abilities measured by an aptitude test are less tied to specific educational experiences than those measured by achievement tests.

Aptitude Defined

More precisely, we can define aptitude as "the ability to acquire a behavior or skill given the appropriate opportunity to learn." The phrase "ability to learn" indicates that the individual already possesses certain prerequisite skills or behaviors, while the term "acquire" denotes the emphasis on future performance. The phrase "behavior or skill" implies that diverse abilities of varying breadth may be relevant; however, we generally talk about aptitude in quite broad terms—e.g., aptitude for mathematics, aptitude for languages, mechanical aptitude, academic aptitude. Finally, "given the appropriate opportunity to learn" signifies that the performance implied by the aptitude will not be manifested unless the appropriate training is provided. Thus, for example, a student with "musical aptitude" would not become an accomplished musician without the necessary training.

Two aspects of this definition have frequently been misunderstood. First, what *is* an aptitude? Traditionally psychologists have described human abilities in terms of clusters of interrelated (intercorrelated) behaviors and characteristics called *traits*. Thus when we say someone is honest, we mean that he manifests a set of behaviors and characteristics that, in our society, we call "honesty." Similarly, to say that a person has "mathematical aptitude" means nothing more than that he possesses a set of abilities and behaviors which characterize persons who (1) find learning mathematics easier than most persons and/or (2) can learn more complex mathematics than most persons.[1] An aptitude is no more nor less than these intercorrelated behaviors.

The other aspect that has caused misunderstanding is the genetic bases of aptitudes. Performance on any test is a function of three factors: (1) the person's genetic endowment, (2) his life experience prior to the testing, and (3) the conditions of the testing. Because performance on most aptitude tests is quite stable over time, many persons have assumed that aptitudes are deter-

---

[1] Similarly, when we say that a person has "no aptitude" we do not mean that he cannot learn anything in the area, but that he will experience more difficulty and learn more slowly and/or to a lesser degree of proficiency than most persons.

mined primarily by genetic factors. While there is no doubt that genetic factors do influence aptitudes, there is also no doubt that they are also strongly influenced by environmental factors. One reason that aptitude often appears immutable is that most persons' life experiences are relatively constant; thus environmental factors do not have full opportunity to express themselves. When environmental conditions change radically, aptitudes may also change significantly.[2]

Intelligence Tests

Probably no other type of psychological test is so widely known, or so misunderstood, as the intelligence or "IQ" test. Although the term "intelligence test" is uncritically applied to various mental ability tests, it is most properly applied to tests that measure overall or global mental ability, adaptability in new situations, and ability to learn new and different materials. In other words, the concept of intelligence is broader than "school learning" and applies to all situations requiring mental or intellectual ability.

Present-day intelligence tests derive from the work of Alfred Binet in France around the turn of the century. Given the task of identifying slow learners in the Paris schools, Binet developed a test that departed from the then current practices by using complex tasks as test items, attempting to measure general mental development rather than separate faculties, and evaluating performance in terms of age scales.

The most direct descendant of Binet's test, among currently used tests, is the *Stanford-Binet Intelligence Scale*. This test, which was developed by Lewis Terman and Maud Merrill at Stanford University, was first introduced into the United States in 1916 and has since undergone several revisions, the latest being publication of Form L–M in 1960.

The test covers an age range from two years to (superior) adults but is most appropriate for younger children. It is individually administered to each child, with items being grouped by age levels. At the preschool levels, items stress the ability to follow directions, identification of common objects and parts of the body, memory, and sensory-motor and perceptual skills. By about age six

---

[2] For a further discussion of this issue see Anastasi, 1958; Bloom, 1964; Guilford, 1967; Hunt, 1961; and Jensen, 1969.

the emphasis shifts to verbal skills (e.g., vocabulary, analogies, similarities and differences), perceptual and verbal discriminations, and simple quantitative skills. At older ages, the item content becomes more verbal and more abstract. On the whole, the test is heavily weighted with verbal material, with quantitative skills playing a relative minor role. (Some examples of the types of items on the Stanford-Binet are listed in Exhibit 7.1).

EXHIBIT 7.1

DESCRIPTION OF ITEMS ON THE STANFORD-BINET INTELLIGENCE SCALE

The following descriptions indicate the type of items appearing at several age levels on the Stanford-Binet.

Year V
1. Picture completion: Man. Child elaborates an incomplete drawing of a man by drawing in details.
2. Paper folding: Triangle. Fold paper in imitation of examiner's pattern.
3. Definitions. Correctly define two (of three) common objects.
4. Copying a square. Draw an acceptable square (with pattern in view).
5. Pictorial Similarities and Differences II. Indicate whether pairs of pictured objects are alike or different.
6. Patience: Rectangles. Construct a rectangle from two cut-out pieces.

Year VIII
1. Vocabularly. Correctly define 8 words (from a 45-word list).
2. Memory for Stories. Answer questions on story that examiner reads (child has copy of story during reading but not during questioning).
3. Verbal Absurdities I. Recognizing absurdities in a statement.
4. Similarities and Differences. Telling how two related objects are alike and how they are different.
5. Comprehension IV. Indicate appropriate course of action in real-life situation or causes of natural phenomena.
6. Naming the Days of the Week. Questions to see if child knows the order of days.

Year XI
1. Memory for Designs I. Drawing a geometric design from memory.
2. Verbal Absurdities IV. (Same type as VIII–3).
3. Abstract Words II. Defining (three) abstract concepts.

EXHIBIT 7.1 (Continued)

4. Memory for Sentences II. Word-for-word repetition of spoken sentences.
5. Problem Situation II. Inferring facts from a short statement.
6. Similarities: Three things. Indicate the basis of similarity of three related objects.

Year XIV

1. Vocabulary. Correctly define 17 (of 45) words.
2. Induction. Discovering rule that allows you to predict results of folding and cutting paper in certain ways.
3. Reasoning I. Deduction of a conclusion from set of facts.
4. Ingenuity I. Problems of type, "How do I obtain 2 quarts of water if I have only an 8 quart and a 3 quart can?"
5. Orientation: Direction I. Ascertaining direction after a series of verbal changes in orientation.
6. Reconciliation of Opposites. In what way are two, apparently dissimilar, objects related?

Source: Reproduced with permission of Houghton Mifflin Company.

Although only one index of performance (a total score) is used, scores are reported in two ways. Each child's performance is expressed as a mental age, that is, the age of the average child that his performance best typifies. This score, in turn, is converted into a measure of relative performance among children of his age, the intelligence quotient or IQ. Originally a ratio IQ was used, but now scores are reported on a normalized standard score scale with mean = 100 and standard deviation = 16 IQ points. Performance, therefore, can be interpreted on a development scale (the mental age) or as a measure of relative "brightness" (the IQ). Thus an IQ of 100 is average for any age level, an IQ of 132 is two standard deviations above the mean, and so on.

Because the Stanford-Binet had several weaknesses as a measure of adult intelligence, David Wechsler has developed several intelligence tests primarily for adults, including the *Wechsler Adult Intelligence Scale* (*WAIS*). Of more interest to educators is the fact that he has also developed two tests that are applicable to school-aged children: the *Wechsler Intelligence Scale for Children* (*WISC*), applicable to the age range 5–15, and a relatively new scale, the *Wechsler Preschool and Primary Scale of Intelligence* (*WPPSI*), which covers only the limited age range four to six and a half years, the critical years when children are first starting formal educational programs.

Like the Stanford-Binet, the Wechsler scales are individually administered and report scores as a deviation IQ (however, with $\overline{X} = 100$ and $s = 15$). There is, however, one major difference; the Wechsler items are arranged by subtests rather than age levels and are divided into two major sections, each yielding an IQ. The Verbal scales, which are comparable to the Binet items, measure vocabulary, general information, arithmetic, comprehension, and similar skills. The Performance scales, in contrast, emphasize perceptual and other nonverbal skills such as making designs with blocks according to a pattern, assembling puzzles, and identifying missing details in pictures. The idea of the Performance scale is to obtain a measure of intellectual ability not confounded with verbal and "book-learning" skills.

Many other tests of intellectual ability are also on the market. Some are designed for infants or preschool children; these are heavily weighted with perceptual and sensory motor skills. Others are performance tests which minimize the role of verbal factors. Because their individual administration makes the Binet and Wechsler infeasible for testing large numbers of persons, many group intelligence tests have been developed. These tests generally consist of certain types of items: vocabulary and its variations, general information, simple arithmetic, verbal and nonverbal reasoning. These tests, of course, use a paper-and-pencil format and alternative-choice items.

Scholastic Aptitude Tests

The tests of intellectual ability commonly used in educational settings are most precisely called scholastic aptitude or academic aptitude tests. Although the content and format of scholastic aptitude tests closely parallel group intelligence tests, they differ in several fundamental ways. Group intelligence tests are designed to measure a trait of intelligence; scholastic aptitude tests are designed to predict success in academic programs. Thus the appropriate validation procedure for intelligence tests is construct validity, while criterion-related validity is paramount for scholastic aptitude tests. And, although the content of items on scholastic aptitude tests will be directly relevant to the educational setting, items must also pass an empirical test of predicting academic performance if they are to be included on the test.

Scholastic aptitude tests are, without exception, paper-and-pencil tests. Items are usually in an alternative-choice format and, except in the primary grades, are confined to verbal and mathematical materials. Performance will usually be reported as a total score and, possibly, two or three part scores, the most common distinction being between verbal and quantitative skills. Different forms of the test will be developed for various age levels.

Some widely used academic aptitude tests are listed in Appendix B. A more detailed descriptive example is given in Exhibit 7.2.

EXHIBIT 7.2

DESCRIPTION OF A SCHOLASTIC APTITUDE TEST
Lorge-Thorndike Intelligence Tests
Multi-level Edition

Publisher: Houghton Mifflin Company

Purpose: Designed as a test of abstract intelligence, the ability to work with ideas, and the relationships among ideas; used for planning and guiding educational experiences.

Levels: The Multi-level edition contains eight overlapping levels in one reusable test booklet; suggested levels are grades 3, 4, 5, 6, 7, 8–9, 10–11, and 12–13, but these levels can be altered to fit abilities of students in a particular school system. Tests can also be purchased in separate single-level editions.

Forms: There are two forms at each level. Can be hand or machine scored; publisher provides machine-scoring services and summary reports.

Content: Test is divided into Verbal and Nonverbal sections. Verbal section includes Vocabulary, Verbal Classification, Sentence Completion, Arithmetic Reasoning, and Verbal Analogies items; each section is 7 minutes long for total writing time of 35 minutes. Nonverbal section includes Pictorial Classification, Pictorial Analogy, and Numerical Relationship items; each section is 9 minutes long for a total time of 27 minutes. (Examples of items are shown in Figure 7.1.)

Scores and Norms: The following scores can be reported, by level, for Verbal and Nonverbal sections separately: Intelligence Quotients (IQ's), Grade Percentiles (percentiles within grades), Grade Equivalents, and Age Equivalents. Norms are based on approximately 19,000 students at each level chosen from communities stratified by size, family income level, and educational level. Scores can be equated to scores on Iowa Tests of Basic Skills and Tests of Academic Progress, published by same company.

Supplemental Tests: Besides the separate level editions there are a College Level and a Primary Battery.

EXHIBIT 7.2 (*Continued*)
College Edition. Level H of the Multi-level edition; standardized on high school seniors; for use in grades 12–13.
Primary Battery. Two levels (K–1, 2–3); two forms at each level; subtests are Oral Vocabulary (definitions and functions), Pictorial Classification (simple relationships), and Pictorial Pairing (more complex relationships); no time limits.
Evaluation: Tests are carefully constructed and normed and are quite reliable. Validity evidence based on selection of items to measure intellectual abilities, correlations with established tests and ability to predict academic performance. (See Mehrens & Lehmann, 1969, pp. 91–101 for a more detailed evaluation.)

Item content is quite standard. Practically all tests strongly emphasize vocabulary, which is the best single index of academic aptitude. Vocabulary items may be simple word meaning items or variations such as analogies items, same-opposites (synonyms, antonyms), sentence completion items (select the appropriate word to complete a sentence), or, in the primary grades, picture vocabulary. Numerical ability items are also included on most tests, either as simple computational items or as items requiring some mathematical reasoning and/or problem-solving skill. Less universal, but still quite common, are reading comprehension items (the student reads a paragraph, then answers questions pertaining to the paragraph), and reasoning items, such as verbal or nonverbal analogies and number series problems (e.g., What number is next in the sequence 1 . . . 4 . . . 9 . . . 16 . . .?). Sometimes other item types—e.g., general information (What is the population of the world?) or tool skills, such as graph interpretation—are also included. Some examples of items from scholastic aptitude tests are shown in Figure 7.1.

The logic of scholastic aptitude tests is probably nowhere better shown than by *college admissions tests.* These tests—of which there are two major representatives, the *Scholastic Aptitude Test* and the *ACT* battery—are designed to provide an estimate of students' potential for college work, independent of his high school performance. Although these tests have been roundly criticized (by, e.g., Hoffman, 1962; Black, 1963), the fact remains that they do predict academic success in college (that is, they have criterion-related validity) and thus aid colleges to select students. Similar tests are available for several professional fields, e.g., the *Graduate Record Examination,* the *Medical College Admissions Test,* the *National Teachers Examination.*

FIGURE 7.1

EXAMPLES OF ITEMS FROM SCHOLASTIC AFTITUDE TESTS: LORGE-THORNDIKE INTELLIGENCE ˉ ESTS, MULTI-LEVEL EDITION

Verbal items:
Vocabulary

For each exercise in this test you are to read the word in dark type at the beginning of each exercise. Then, from the five words that follow you are to choose the word that has the same meaning or most nearly the same meaning as the word in dark type. Look at sample exercise 0.

0. loud   A quick   B noisy   C hard   D heavy   E weak

The word which has most nearly the same meaning as **loud** is **noisy.** The letter in front of **noisy** is **B,** so on your answer sheet make a heavy black pencil mark in the **B** answer space for exercise 0.

Verbal classification

For each exercise in this test, a series of words is given in dark type. You are to figure out how the words in dark type are alike, then you are to choose the one word among the five on the line below that belongs with the words in dark type. Look at sample exercise 0.

0. rose   daisy   violet

A red   B garden   C sweet   D grow   E lily

All the words in dark type are the names of flowers. Of the five words on the line below, only **lily** is the name of a flower. The letter in front of **lily** is **E,** so on your answer sheet make a heavy black pencil mark in the **E** answer space for exercise 0.

Now look at exercise 00. Think in what way the words in dark type go together. Then find the word on the line below that belongs with them.

00. go   run   walk   move

F think   G dream   H march   J sing   K seem

The right answer is **march.** The letter in front of **march** is **H** so on your answer sheet make a heavy black pencil mark in the **H** answer space for exercise 00.

Sentence completion

In each exercise in this test, a word has been left out of a sentence. Read the sentence carefully; then, from the five words that follow, choose the one word that will make the best, the truest, and the most sensible complete sentence. Look at sample exercise 0.

0. Hot weather comes in the ――――――.

A fall   B night   C summer   D winter   E snow

The best answer is **summer.** The word **summer** makes the best, truest, and most sensible complete sentence. The letter in front of summer is **C,** so on your answer sheet make a heavy black pencil mark in the **C** answer space for exercise 0.

FIGURE 7.1 (Continued)

Arithmetic reasoning

In this test you are to work some arithmetic problems. After each problem are four possible answers and a fifth choice, "none of these," meaning that the correct answer is not given.

Work each problem and compare your answer with the four possible answers. If the correct answer is given, fill in the space on the answer sheet that has the same letter as the right answer. If the correct answer is not given, fill in the space on the answer sheet that has the same letter as "none of these." Look at sample exercise 0.

0. If candy costs a cent a piece, how much will nine pieces cost?

    A 1¢   B 7¢   C 8¢   D 9¢   E none of these

The correct answer is 9¢. The letter in front of 9¢ is **D** so on your answer sheet make a heavy black pencil mark in the **D** answer space for exercise 0.

Now look at sample exercise 00.

00. Mrs. Jones bought a pound of potatoes for 10¢ and a pound of spinach for 15¢. How much did she spend?

    F 5¢   G 10¢   H 15¢   J 20¢   K none of these

The correct answer is 25¢. The answers at **F, G, H,** and **J** are wrong, so you would choose "none of these" as your correct answer. The letter in front of "none of these" is **K** so on your answer sheet make a heavy black pencil mark in the **K** answer space for exercise 00.

Verbal analogies

For each exercise in this test, a pair of words is given that are related to each other in some way. Look at the first two words and figure out how they are related to each other. Then, from the five words on the line below, choose the word that is related to the third word in the same way. Look at sample exercise 0.

0. laugh → happy : cry →

    A wonder   B sad   C hide   D lost   E rough

The right answer is **sad** because you **laugh** when you are **happy** and you **cry** when you are **sad**. The letter before **sad** is **B** so on your answer sheet make a heavy black pencil mark in the **B** answer space for exercise 0.

Now look at exercise 00.

00. chair → sit : bed →

    F lie   G bedroom   H night   J crib   K tired

The right answer is **lie** because you **sit** in a **chair** and you **lie** in **bed**. The letter in front of **lie** is **F** so on your answer sheet make a heavy black pencil mark in the **F** answer space for exercise 00.

FIGURE 7.1 (*Continued*)

Nonverbal items:
Pictorial classification

For each exercise in this test, a series of drawings is given which are alike in a certain way. You are to figure out in what way the drawings are alike. Then you are to find the drawing at the right that goes with the first group. Look at sample exercise 0. The first three drawings in the row are alike in a certain way. Find the drawing at the right that goes with the first three.

The first three drawings are alike in that each has four sides and no lines inside it. The drawing at the right that goes with them is at **D**. It has four sides and no lines inside it. Make a heavy black pencil mark in the **D** answer space for exercise 0.

Now look at exercise 00. Find the drawing at the right that goes with the first three.

The first three drawings are alike in that they are all circles and they are getting smaller. At the right the only one that is a circle and is still smaller is at **H**. Make a heavy black pencil mark in the **H** answer space for exercise 00.

Pictorial analogies

In each exercise in this test, the first two drawings go together in a certain way. You are to figure out how the first two go together, then find the drawing at the right that goes with the third drawing in the same way that the second goes with the first. Look at sample exercise 0.

The first two drawings go together because you wear a glove on your hand; therefore the right answer is the shoe because you wear a shoe on your foot. The letter in front of the drawing of the shoe is **C** so make a heavy black pencil mark in the **C** answer space for exercise 0.

Now look at exercise 00. Find the drawing at the right that goes with the third drawing in the same way as the second drawing goes with the first drawing.

The right answer is **K**, because the little circle at **K** goes with the little square just as the big circle goes with the big square. Make a heavy black pencil mark in the **K** answer space for exercise 00.

FIGURE 7.1 (Continued)

Numerical relationships

For each exercise in this test a series of numbers or letters is given in a certain order. You are to figure out the order (or way) in which the series of numbers or letters is arranged, then find the number or letter at the right that should come next. Look at sample exercise 0.

0.   1   3   5   7   9 →   A 10   B 11   C 12   D 13   E 14

In the series of numbers, 1 3 5 7 9, each number is 2 more than the number before it, therefore, the next number in the series should be 11. The letter in front of 11 is **B** so make a heavy black pencil mark in the **B** answer space for exercise 0.

Now look at exercise 00. Find the number that should come next.

00.   5   5   4   4   3 →   F 1   G 2   H 3   J 4   K 5

The next number should be 3, so make a heavy black pencil mark in the **H** answer space for exercise 00.

Note: The items illustrated above are the practice items from the test.

Source: Reproduced with permission of Houghton Mifflin Company, © 1964.

Multiple Aptitude Tests

General intelligence and scholastic aptitude tests were based on the assumption that the various facets of intellectual ability are closely interrelated. Many American psychologists, however, subscribe to an alternative view—that intellectual structure is best described by a small number of relatively broad, yet quite independent abilities. Although there is not complete agreement as to what these abilities are, those which have been identified in a number of studies[3] include: verbal comprehension—knowledge of word meanings and relationships between words; number—performing simple arithmetic computations rapidly and accurately; perceptual speed—quick and accurate perception of details; spatial—ability to visualize and mentally manipulate geometric patterns in space; rote memory—immediate recall of nonmeaningful materials; word fluency—ability to supply many words; and reasoning (induction)—ability to extract rules.

Several published tests illustrate this approach to the measurement of abilities. As would be expected, they are actually test

[3] Most studies of the structure of intellect use a statistical technique called *factor analysis*. Operationally this technique involves administering a large number of tests to a group of subjects, intercorrelating all pairs of scores, analyzing the intercorrelation matrix, and extracting the (minimum number of) factors needed to account for the pattern of intercorrelations among tests.

EXHIBIT 7.3
DESCRIPTION OF THE DIFFERENTIAL APTITUDE TESTS

Verbal Reasoning—measures ability to understand verbal concepts, to abstract and generalize, not just verbal fluency; uses special analogies format (two blanks per item) and diverse content; cf. the verbal comprehension factor (see text).

Numerical Ability—measures understanding of numerical relationships and facility with numbers; problems are simple computations, unconfounded with verbal content or reasoning (word problems); cf. the numerical ability factor.

Abstract Reasoning—items are series of diagrams which change in a systematic manner, task is to find the operating principle and use it to predict next pattern in sequence; no premium on visual acuity or verbal content; cf. the reasoning factor.

Space Relations—measures ability to mentally manipulate objects in three-dimensional space; item format is combination of two common types: (1) the ability to visualize a constructed object from a pattern, and (2) ability to visualize objects rotated in space; cf. the space factor.

Mechanical Reasoning—tests understanding of mechanical and physical principles; items pictorially present a mechanical situation and ask a simple question regarding situation; only simple common mechanisms used.

Clerical Speed and Accuracy—measures speed and accuracy of perceptual response; items require comparison of combinations of letters or numbers; low difficulty but heavy premium on speed; cf. perceptual speed factor.

Language Usage—contains two parts, each yielding separate score; Spelling involves recognizing misspelled words; Sentences, recognizing errors in grammar, punctuation, and word usage; is an achievement test but included in battery as it measures abilities that are important in many vocational and educational fields.

batteries with separate tests measuring different abilities; hence the title, multiple aptitude tests. Of these batteries, the *Differential Aptitude Tests* (*DAT*) are probably the most widely used in education.

The DAT consists of seven tests, five of which measure characteristics similar to the factors mentioned above. (See Exhibit 7.3 for a description of the tests.) The other two are a test of an important vocational aptitude (Mechanical Reasoning) and an achievement test (Language Usage); both were included because of their relevance for vocational counseling and educational planning. In addition, the combined score on two tests (Verbal Reasoning + Numerical Ability) is used as an index of academic aptitude.

The DAT was designed to be a counseling tool. Thus, although each test can be administered and interpreted independently, the recommended procedure is to administer the entire battery and, by considering the test profile, identify students' relative strengths and weaknesses, in both academic and vocational abilities.

Special Aptitudes

There also are a number of tests of more limited scope, tests that measure relatively specific aptitudes and abilities.[4] Many of these tests measure vocational aptitudes; the Mechanical Reasoning and Clerical Speed and Accuracy sections of the DAT are good illustrations of (paper-and-pencil) mechanical and clerical aptitude tests, respectively. (Figure 7.2 shows the type of items used.) Other tests are available for academic fields—e.g., foreign languages—and in music and art, areas where only limited success in measuring aptitudes has been attained.

CREATIVITY. One ability that has attracted widespread interest among educators is creativity. Research has been directed toward identifying the characteristics of creative persons, the conditions which foster creativity, and the dimensions of creative behavior. Studies have been conducted both within the classroom setting (e.g., Getzels and Jackson, 1962; Torrance, 1962) and as part of an attempt to develop a theory of intellectual structure (Guilford, 1967).

What is meant by creativity? Although there is not complete agreement on a definition—as, indeed, there is not agreement on the definitions for other traits, even one as widely used as intelligence—several common threads appear in the various definitions. Thus we can define creativity as the ability to think divergently, to produce a variety of original (but rational) responses.

This definition, however, will not be sufficient unless it differentiates creativity from other abilities. For example, if students who score high on creativity measures also score high on traditional intelligence tests, we are not measuring two distinct abilities;

---

[4] The best compendium on vocational aptitude tests is Super and Crites, 1962.

FIGURE 7.2

EXAMPLES OF ITEMS FROM VOCATIONAL APTITUDE TESTS: THREE SECTIONS FROM THE DIFFERENTIAL APTITUDE TESTS.

MECHANICAL REASONING

DIRECTIONS

This test consists of a number of pictures and questions about those pictures. Look at Example X on this page to see just what to do. Example X shows a picture of two men carrying a machine part on a board and asks, "Which man has the heavier load? If equal, mark C." Man "B" has the heavier load because the weight is closer to him than to man "A," so on the separate Answer Sheet you would fill in the space under B, like this ⟶

Now look at Example Y. The question asks, "Which weighs more? If equal, mark C." As the scale is perfectly balanced, "A" and "B" must weigh the same, so you would blacken the space under C on your separate Answer Sheet, like this ⟶

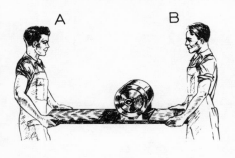

X

Which man has the heavier load?

(If equal, mark C.)

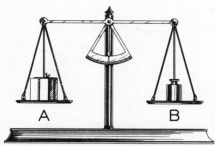

Y

Which weighs more?

(If equal, mark C.)

On the following pages there are more pictures and questions. Read each question carefully, look at the picture, and mark your answer on the separate Answer Sheet. Do not forget that there is a third choice for every question.

FIGURE 7.2 (*Continued*)

SPACE RELATIONS

DIRECTIONS

This test consists of forty patterns which can be folded into figures. For each pattern, five figures are shown. You are to decide which of these figures can be made from the pattern shown. The pattern always shows the outside of the figure. Here is an example:

EXAMPLE X

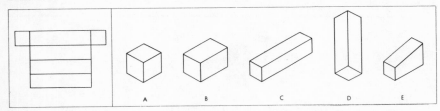

Which of these five figures — A, B, C, D, E — can be made from the pattern in Example X? A and B certainly cannot be made; they are not the right shape. C and D **are** correct both in shape and size. You cannot make E from this pattern.

— In the test there will always be a row of five figures for each pattern.

— In every row there is at least one correct figure.

— Usually **more** than one is correct. In fact, in some cases, all five may be correct.

Now look at the pattern for Example Y and the five choices for it. Note that when the pattern is folded, the figure must have two **gray** surfaces. One of these is a large surface which could be **either** the top or bottom of a box. The other is a small surface which would be one end of the box.

FIGURE 7.2 (*Continued*)

SPEED AND ACCURACY

DIRECTIONS

This is a test to see how quickly and accurately you can compare letter and number combinations. On the following pages are groups of these combinations; each Test Item contains five. These same combinations appear after the number for each Test Item on the separate Answer Sheet, but they are in a different order. You will notice that in each Test Item one of the five is **underlined**. You are to look at the **one** combination which is underlined, find the **same** one after that item number on the separate **Answer** Sheet, and fill in the space under it.

These examples are correctly done. Note that the combination on the Answer Sheet must be exactly the same as the one in the Test Item.

TEST ITEMS •   SAMPLE OF ANSWER SHEET

V. AB	AC	AD	AE	AF
W. aA	aB	BA	Ba	Bb
X. A7	7A	B7	7B	AB
Y. Aa	Ba	bA	BA	bB
Z. 3A	3B	33	B3	BB

	AC	AE	AF	AB	AD
V	:::::	:::::	:::::	▬	.:::::
W	BA	Ba	Bb	aA	aB
X	7 B	B7	AB	7A	A7
Y	Aa	bA	bB	Ba	BA
Z	BB	3B	B3	3A	33

If you finish the items in Part I before time is called, check your work. Do not turn to Part II until you are told to do so. Work as fast as you can.

Note: These are practice items from the test.

rather we would be measuring two manifestations of the same ability. Although the evidence is not definitive, it does appear that the better creativity measures are tapping abilities not measured by other tests.

How, then, do we measure creativity? One approach is to have experts rate creative performances or products—poems, paintings, designs. But this approach only evaluates developed talents. In attempts to identify creative potential, both Torrance and Guilford, among others, have developed paper-and-pencil tests of creativity. These tests include several types of items: for example, measures of verbal fluency (e.g., the ability to produce synonyms), listing possible uses for objects (What are the various uses for a brick?), producing drawings or designs from a specified stimulus (usually a simple line drawing), listing the possible causes or consequences of an act.

The measurement of creativity presents certain psychometric problems. For one, the test format must allow the student to construct a response rather than just choose among alternatives. This fact, coupled with the necessity for ruling out obviously irrational or trivial responses, makes objective scoring difficult. Second, because creativity is strongly influenced by the particular stimulus situation and motivational and personality characteristics, reliability is often lower than on other types of tests. And, finally, because by definition creative responses are original responses, obtaining appropriate normative and validity data is often quite difficult.

Implications for Education

Having described the various approaches to measuring intellectual abilities, we will now raise several questions regarding their effective use in education.

First, are the various intellectual abilities closely related? Although the theoretical research indicates that there are distinct abilities, thus supporting the multiple aptitude approach, results from applied studies and practical considerations point up the usefulness of the general ability approach (see, e.g., McNemar, 1964). Furthermore, achievement and ability are highly intercorrelated—not a surprising fact considering that both measure the results of learning, using tests having similar content (e.g., word meanings, arithmetic, general information) and format (paper-and-pencil, alternative-choice items.)

In general, the more heterogeneous the group, the higher the intercorrelations between abilities; the more homogeneous the group, the more apparent independence of abilities. This generalization can explain the controversy over the relationship between creativity and intelligence. That is, over the entire population there is a relationship between these two abilities, but within more homogeneous groups, say children with IQ's over 115, the two abilities are relatively independent.

Second, what do measures of intellectual ability contribute to the educational process? Certainly their main use has been as aids in the selection and placement of students in academic programs. In this effort they have been moderately, but not overwhelmingly, successful; validity coefficients for predicting academic criteria, such as grades, usually falling in the .40–.70 range (Goslin, 1963; Lavin, 1965). This generalization requires several qualifications: (1) there are wide differences between schools, with validity being quite high in some and near zero in others; (2) prediction is more accurate in academic courses, e.g., English and math, than in other areas; (3) scores on achievement tests can be predicted more accurately than grades assigned by teachers; (4) general ability measures are as accurate predictors as weighted combinations of special abilities; and (5) using multiple aptitude tests as differential predictors (that is, using numerical ability tests to predict performance in mathematics, vocabulary to predict in English) results in only moderate gains in predictive efficiency.

Several other considerations also pertain. As past performance is usually the best single predictor of future performance, achievement tests are usually as good, or better, predictors of future academic performance in the same field than are academic ability measures. And, as Gough (1965) has mentioned, there is more than "one true path to grace"; that is, the same outcome can be accomplished in various ways. For example, studies have shown that highly creative and highly intelligent children may achieve at comparable levels, even though using different talents and approaches. Then, too, even a moderately effective instrument, which will make some mistakes when classifying individuals, can be useful if its effectiveness is viewed over an entire group or in comparison to other available techniques. And it has been suggested (Rosenthal & Jacobson, 1968) that children's academic performance may be a function of teachers' expectations as well as their ability level.

Third, are scholastic aptitude tests fair to all children? This issue is often phrased as a definitive statement—that tests do have a middle-class bias and are thus unfair to children from lower socioeconomic classes and minority groups—rather than as a question. Of course, the key issue is what is meant by "fair." If by "fair" we mean: Are tests constructed so that all groups will obtain the same average scores? the answer is No. If by "fair" we mean: Do certain groups of children obtain lower than average scores? the answer is Yes. If by "fair" we mean: Do tests predict academic performance equally well for middle-class and minority groups? the answer, although far from definitive, is Usually. If by "fair" we mean: Are test scores sometimes used, however incorrectly, to support educational practices that discriminate against minority group members? again we would have to answer Yes, for tests are certainly misused at times.

Academic ability tests, like all other tests, reflect students' past experiences and opportunities to learn. If these opportunities have been limited, as certainly they have for many children from minority groups and lower socioeconomic classes, this disadvantage will be reflected, as indeed it is, in lower test scores. And, as all learning is based on past learning, the child will also be at a disadvantage in academic situations, a fact that the test score points out. Thus, in one sense, it is not the test that is unfair, but life itself. Misuse and misinterpretations of ability tests occur when we forget that (1) test scores are the result of the child's total experience, but particularly his opportunities to learn, and (2) test scores are not immutable indices, but rather only indicate the present level of ability.

This leads us to a fourth question: What can be done to improve the intellectual skills of children, in particular, minority group and disadvantaged children? Most educational psychologists interpret the evidence on mental growth, particularly its rapid increase in early years and relative stability thereafter, as indicating that the most crucial period is the preschool years (see, e.g., Hunt, 1961; Bloom, 1964). Although educational psychologists are agreed that the best time for developing basic intellectual skills is the preschool years, and that intensive, not short-term, training is needed,[5] they disagree considerably on the form and content of the training required.

MEASURING TYPICAL PERFORMANCE

The tests that we have discussed have been, without exception, measures of maximal performance; that is, they were designed to obtain an estimate of the student's best possible performance. The

---

[5] See Jensen, 1969, and also the replies to Jensen in the Spring and Summer, 1969, issues of the *Harvard Educational Review* for a controversial discussion of the effectiveness of current programs and the broader issues surrounding compensatory education.

set for maximal performance was engendered by the test directions ("attempt every item even if unsure of the correct answer"), by rewarding good performance (e.g., by higher grades), and by the general American ethic of trying one's best.

In addition to measures of maximal performance, there are tests which measure typical performance. Here we are interested in the person's habitual behavior—we do not want to know if he can be the life of the party, but whether he usually is; we do not want to know if he is sometimes depressed or blue, but rather how frequently he is. Tests of typical performance, therefore, usually measure personality characteristics rather than achievement or abilities.

Methods

There are three approaches to measuring typical performance: self-report inventories, projective techniques, and situational methods.

The *self-report inventory*, as its name implies, uses as responses students' reports of their typical behavior, feelings, or attitudes. As no other person has as much opportunity to observe his behavior as the individual himself, it is assumed that the most complete description can be obtained by asking the individual. Of course, we must also assume that the individual will give an unbiased report; often a tenuous assumption. However, scales have been developed to measure the magnitude of these response biases, and are included on most self-report inventories.

The self-report method is the technique used in the construction of personality and vocational interest inventories. The usual procedure is to administer a large number of items (statements) and ask the student to indicate whether the statement describes him. For example, a personality inventory might include statements such as:

I frequently feel blue or depressed.
At a party I like to become acquainted with persons I do not know.
Most people will take advantage of you if you don't watch out.

An inventory usually contains several scales, each measuring a different personality trait. These scales may have been developed by empirical keying (including items that discriminate between persons who do and do not exhibit a trait) or by homogeneous keying (finding sets of items that are highly intercorrelated).

The second method, *projective techniques,* is based on the fact that a person when confronted with a novel or ambiguous situation will impose some structure on the situation. His method of imposing structure and the type of structure are used as a base for inferring personality characteristics. The prime example of this approach is the *Rorschach (Inkblot) Method.*

In contrast, *situational methods* attempt to make the testing situation more realistic by observing the person's reactions and behavior when he is involved in a problem-solving situation, usually one involving interpersonal relationships. For example, we might ask a group of candidates to organize an advertising campaign; by observing their approach to the problem and their interactions with the other members of the group, we could rate them along a number of personality dimensions, e.g., leadership, dominance, self-confidence, extraversion.

Uses in Education

The use for personality measures in education is to help us better understand the individual learner, either to identify attitudes and personality characteristics that may be interfering with his learning, or values and interests that may affect his educational plans.

Of the various measures of typical performance, interest inventories would seem to have most potential value in education. These inventories provide two types of information: Some compare a student's interests to those of people engaged in specific occupations (e.g., electrical engineers, physicians, retail sales clerks, plumbers) while others measure interest in broad occupational areas (e.g., science, mechanical areas, sales). Several of the major inventories—e.g., the *Strong Vocational Interest Blank,* The *Kuder Occupational Interest Survey* and the *Minnesota Vocational Interest Inventory*—now provide both types of scores. Although interest inventories may provide useful information for vocational and educational planning, they should be used with caution in public schools, as empirical evidence indicates that vocational interests generally do not stabilize until around age twenty.

Other types of personality measures, with the possible exception of study habits inventories, would seem to be of more limited value in education. In fact, given the present state of the art of personality measurement and the fact that the same information can frequently be obtained from observing the child in the classroom and in his personal interactions, the classroom teacher would be well advised to make no use of standardized personality measures, leaving their use to counselors and school psychologists, if they are to be used at all.

SOURCES OF INFORMATION

In the past two chapters we have mentioned only a handful of the hundreds of standardized tests. Thus it would be well to indicate where further information about available tests might be found.

The test user has various sources that he might consult: textbooks on psychological and educational testing, journals in psychology and education, college instructors teaching measurement courses, high school counselors and school psychologists, and test publishers' catalogs. Two particularly helpful sources are the books by Super & Crites (1962) and Mehrens & Lehmann (1969).

The major references, however, are a series of publications edited by O. K. Buros. One, *Tests in Print* (Buros, 1961), is a listing of all published tests. Another, which is the core of the series, is the *Mental Measurements Yearbooks*. These are published periodically—the fifth edition in 1959, the sixth edition in 1965—and contain a wealth of information about published tests: e.g., the publisher, cost, time limits, sections and scores, age ranges, references to the test. In addition, the Yearbooks contain critical reviews of new and widely used tests written by both psychometricians and test users. Third, Buros has recently begun publishing monographs collating reviews and references of tests in a particular area—*e.g.*, personality tests, reading tests. All test users should be familiar with, and use, these references.

When choosing or evaluating a test, there is no substitute for actually studying the test items and construction and technical characteristics of the test. This can be done by ordering a *specimen set* of the test from the test publisher. A specimen set contains a copy of the test, the answer sheet, scoring keys, and manuals covering development of the test, its administration, scoring and interpretation, and technical data. Before adopting a test, the user should always obtain and study a specimen set.

SUMMARY

In this chapter we have discussed standardized ability and personality measures and their uses in education. After defining aptitude as the ability to acquire a skill or behavior given appropriate training, we discussed four types of measures of intellectual ability: general intelligence tests, scholastic aptitude tests, multiple aptitude tests, and tests of special abilities. Primary emphasis was devoted to scholastic aptitude tests; descriptions of a test battery and typical items were included.

Several questions regarding the use of ability tests were discussed, including the degree of intercorrelation between various intellectual abilities, what outcomes academic ability tests predict, whether tests are unfair to certain groups, and how intellectual skills can be improved.

Measures of typical performance—self-report inventories, projective techniques, and situational methods—were discussed only briefly because of their limited usefulness in educational settings.

Finally, sources of information that can be consulted to obtain information about standardized tests were identified. It was suggested that the user consult the *Mental Measurements Yearbook* and study a specimen set before adopting a test.

REFERENCES

ANASTASI, A. *Differential Psychology*. 3rd ed. New York: The Macmillan Company, 1958.

BLACK, H. *They Shall Not Pass*. New York: William Morrow & Co., Inc., 1963.

BLOOM, B. S. *Stability and Change in Human Characteristics*. New York: John Wiley & Sons, Inc., 1964.

BUROS, O. K. (ed.) *The Fifth Mental Measurements Yearbook*. Highland Park, N.J.: The Gryphon Press, 1959.

BUROS, O. K. *Tests in Print*. Highland Park, N.J.: The Gryphon Press, 1961.

BUROS, O. K. (ed.) *The Sixth Mental Measurements Yearbook*. Highland Park, N.J.: The Gryphon Press, 1965.

BUROS, O. K. (ed.) *Personality Tests and Reviews*. Highland Park, N.J.: The Gryphon Press, 1969.

Buros, O. K. (ed.) *Reading Tests and Reviews*. Highland Park, N.J.: The Gryphon Press, 1969.

Getzels, J. W., and Jackson, P. W. *Creativity and Intelligence: Explorations with Gifted Students*. New York: John Wiley & Sons, Inc., 1962.

Goslin, D. A. *The Search for Ability: Standardized Testing in Social Perspective*. New York: Russell Sage Foundation, 1963.

Gough, H. "Misplaced Emphases in Admissions," *Journal of College Student Personnel*, Vol. 6 (1965), pp. 130–35.

Guilford, J. P. *The Nature of Human Intelligence*. New York: McGraw-Hill Book Co., 1967.

Hoffman, B. *The Tyranny of Testing*. New York: Crowell Collier and Macmillan, Inc., 1962.

Hunt, J. McV. *Intelligence and Experience*. New York: Ronald Press Co., 1961.

Jensen, A. R. "How Much Can We Boost IQ and Scholastic Achievement?" *Harvard Educational Review*, Vol. 39 (1969), pp. 1–123.

Lavin, D. E. *The Prediction of Academic Performance*. New York: Russell Sage Foundation, 1965.

McNemar, Q. "Lost: Our Intelligence. Why?" *American Psychologist*, Vol. 19 (1964), pp. 871–82.

Mehrens, W. A., and Lehmann, I. J. *Standardized Tests in Education*. New York: Holt, Rinehart & Winston, Inc., 1969.

Rosenthal, R., and Jacobson, L. *Pygmalion in the Classroom*. New York: Holt, Rinehart & Winston, Inc., 1968.

Super, D. E., and Crites, J. O. *Appraising Vocational Fitness*. New York: Harper & Row, Publishers, 1962.

Torrance, P. *Guiding Creative Talent*. Englewood Cliffs, N.J.: Prentice-Hall, Inc., 1962.

8

GRADING

Perhaps no educational practice is the subject of as much controversy as grading practices. Opinions as to the proper method of grading vary tremendously. On one extreme is the instructor who feels that stringent grading upholds "standards" and that students should be compared to what, for him, is an absolute standard of excellence. On the other hand, many people argue that grading is inimical to learning and that the only evaluation should be the student's evaluation of his progress in attaining the goals that he himself has set. Most positions between these extremes are also represented in the literature. Thus it is not surprising that one review concluded: ". . . no commonly accepted system [of grading] has emerged from a half century of inquiry." (Smith & Dobbin, 1960, p. 789).

Some Points of Agreement

Although there is much disagreement, there also are numerous points of agreement regarding grading practices. For example, it is obvious that grading practices should be consistent with the educational philosophy and goals of the institution. If well-defined outcomes (goals) are prescribed, then the grading practices should reflect the degree of attainment of these goals. Conversely, if goals are not clearly formulated, then the grading system (and the exams and other measures which grades are based on) will, in effect, set the standards.

A second point of agreement is that any grade should be based on sufficient evidence. The evidence may be from final exams, unit exams and quizzes, laboratory work, written assignments, classroom recitation and discussion, special projects, or other sources. The important point is that sufficient evidence be collected to ensure both the reliability of the grades and that adequate sampling of the domain has been attained (content validity).

Closely related is a third point, that the bases for grading be clearly specified, not only to aid the teacher in determining grades but, more importantly, to indicate to the student the bases on which he is being evaluated. The teacher should specify what performances will (and will not) be used to determine grades, the relative weight given each component, and the bases on which the individual performance will be evaluated. Thus a teacher might tell his students that the final examination will determine 40 percent of the course grade, that the exam will be composed of four essay questions, and that the most important consideration in grading will be the students' ability to integrate factual material and develop general principles.

Fourth, any method for computing grades should be objective and statistically sound. Objective means that trained graders would assign the same grades and that irrelevant factors, such as personality clashes between teacher and student, would not influence grading. Furthermore, the statistical procedures used should accomplish their desired goals. For example, if the final exam is to constitute 40 percent of the grade, the statistical procedures used in combining grades should insure that the final exam is, in fact, weighted as 40 percent of the total. (The statistical aspects of grading will be discussed later in this chapter.)

Fifth, the grading scale should be simple and easy to interpret. The most common grading system in high schools and colleges is the five-step A–B–C–D–F scale, or a variation thereof. Other commonly used systems are percentage scales (1–100 percent), pass-fail systems, and, in elementary schools, general ratings like "satisfactory—needs improvement—unsatisfactory." Needless to say, there are hundreds of variations on each of these systems.

Even the presumed simplicity and meaningfulness of the A–F scale may be more illusory than real. For example, although a C grade is usually defined as indicating "average performance," we could ask: Average by what standard or definition? What level of skill or knowledge is implied by a C grade? Is a C grade at one school comparable to a C at another school? Is a grade of C assigned by one teacher equivalent to another teacher's C grade? Is a C in one course comparable to a C in another subject? and so on.

Finally, grades should be based on positive characteristics— they should indicate the knowledge a student possesses, the skills he has mastered, or what he can do. Although most educators would probably agree to this principle in the abstract, as positive rewards are the most effective reinforcers, it is not necessarily carried through to grading practices.[1] Too often grades emphasize students' deficiencies rather than their strengths.

Functions of Grades

It is unlikely that a practice as much criticized as grading would have survived unless it served some central purpose in the educational process. And grades do serve a variety of purposes, both for individual students and for the institution.

Probably the most debated function of grades is their role as motivators. While almost everyone agrees that grades should not be used as threats, even the process of using grades to reward good performance (i.e., as positive reinforcers) has been criticized. The argument is that grades are extrinsic motivators, and intrinsic motivation is preferable. But, as Ebel (1965) has pointed out, most rewards in this life are extrinsic and, indeed, few enterprises would succeed if they relied solely on intrinsic motivations. We should also note that, although the debate over grades as motivators usually centers on course grades, the cumulative effect of day-to-day evaluations probably has a greater influence on students' motivation, for, in most cases, the final mark merely confirms what the student already knows about the teacher's judgment of the quality of his performance.

Grades are also said to provide necessary feedback to students regarding the effectiveness of their learning. That grades do serve this function is undoubtedly true if we are referring to grades on

---

[1] The author recently encountered a grading system (i.e., report card) which reported only those areas where the student needed improvement and contained no indication of the student's level of achievement, his strong points, or his accomplishments.

individual tests and assignments. Whether course grades also serve this function is highly debatable because they are summary indices which do not directly refer to the quality or correctness of specific responses and, as we indicated in the previous paragraph, the feedback provided by final grades often only confirms what the student already knows. Furthermore, more extensive and helpful feedback can be provided in other manners—e.g., by the instructor's comments on test papers, by student-instructor conferences.

Another purported function of grades is for guiding learning. That is, grades in one course, or segment of a course, can be used to indicate which experiences or programs a student should next undertake. The important variables in planning subsequent learning experiences are the student's degree of mastery of the prior material and the course of his learning in attaining this level. If grades reflect these two variables, uncontaminated by other influences, they can be used for selecting appropriate future experiences; if not, more direct and objective indices should be utilized.

Using a longer range perspective, grades can be valuable information in educational and vocational planning. Several examples illustrate typical situations: Should a high school student who has consistently received D's in mathematics courses be encouraged (or allowed) to take physics? Should a student whose high school record shows an A average in English and history courses and B's and C's in mathematics and sciences enroll in a prelaw or a premedical curriculum in college? What are the chances that a student with above average high school grades but only mediocre scores on academic ability tests will succeed academically at an intellectually competitive liberal arts college and at a less competitive institution? In making these sorts of decisions, teachers' ratings of a student's performance, as indicated by grades, can be useful sources of information.

Besides providing feedback to students, grades are often defended because they provide feedback to parents regarding their children's academic progress. That a set of letters or numbers, assigned by teachers who parents probably know only slightly if at all, on bases that are only vaguely defined, will communicate much valuable information to parents is unlikely. Parent-teacher conversations and the results of standardized achievement batteries would seem to be more valuable methods of providing parents with an understanding of their children's academic progress.

Finally, grades perform some useful administrative functions. As students generally have different teachers each year, a cumulative record of each student's educational progress can be useful to the teacher in understanding the student's previous academic performance; course grades and scores on achievement batteries are two bits of information that should be in this record. At points of transition—for example, from elementary school to junior high school, from high school to college—grade records are frequently used as a basis for admissions and/or placement within particular tracks, programs, or curricula. Grades may also be used for other academic purposes, such as awarding scholarships, and potential employers may want an indication of a student's academic performance. In all these situations, grades or grade averages serve as an index of the student's academic performance.

To recapitulate, grades do serve some necessary functions in education: to provide the student with an indication of the effectiveness of his learning (grades on individual tests or assignments only), as an aid in educational and vocational planning, and as information for a cumulative performance record. Many of the other purported functions of grades can be better handled in other manners or by using other sources of information.

GRADING TESTS AND ASSIGNMENTS

Grading occurs in two situations: (1) when assigning grades to classroom tests and assignments and (2) in the determination of course marks. As course grades (marks) usually are derived from a combination of grades on individual tests and assignments, we shall consider the former first.

The process of assigning a grade to a classroom test generally involves three steps. First, the test is scored and a raw score obtained, usually the total number of points amassed for correct responses. Second, this raw score is transformed into a derived score, such as a percentile ranking. Third, this score is then translated into a letter grade or another type of mark.

However, there are a number of situations where a different procedure is needed—when a English teacher grades themes, a music teacher rates students' ability to sightread and play a passage, an art teacher evaluates students' paintings, a chemistry teacher grades students' laboratory technique or their reports on the experiments they performed, and so on. In each of these examples the teacher is, in essence, rating student performance. Let us, therefore, consider the rating process.

The common thread among all rating scales is that they require an observer to describe an individual's behavior by assigning it to one of a set of prescribed categories or to a position along a continuum. Ratings may be quite broad, as when we make an overall evaluation of a theme or a musical performance, or they may be narrower and apply only to a specific aspect of behavior. Rating categories may indicate amount or level of quality or be descriptive. On most scales, however, the various categories will be assigned numerals corresponding to a (rank) ordering of the categories.

Many ratings in education use, explicitly or implicitly, a *numerical rating scale*. In this procedure, an observer rates performance on a scale consisting of a sequence of defined numerals. For example, a classroom teacher might evaluate students' responses to her questions during a recitation session using a scale:

> 3—(completely) correct.
> 2—generally correct but incomplete or minor error.
> 1—inadequate, lacking an essential element.
> 0—incorrect.

Or an elementary school teacher, when rating maps or charts prepared by her students, might use a scale:

5—complete and technically accurate.
4—no more than two minor errors or omissions.
3—one major error or omission *or* several minor ones.
2—several major errors or omissions and/or numerous minor ones.
1—numerous major errors; used wrong procedure.

Although we do not need to assign numerical values to categories (and, in fact, most teachers probably skip this step and assign marks directly), use of numerical scores facilitates combining scores to obtain course grades.

Another procedure which is widely applicable is rating by *cumulative points,* a procedure analogous to grading problems and essay questions. Here the individual is assigned a score corresponding to the number of designated elements which he displays (see Figure 8.1–A for an example). In some instances, ratings can be assigned by comparing the student's performance to a desig-

FIGURE 8.1
EXAMPLES OF RATING SCALES

A. Examples of graphic rating scales.
[Rater checks scale position which best describes student's behavior.]
A-1. Ability to work independently:

Completes assignments with minimal supervision	Works independently if task clearly structured	Frequently asks questions and advice	Needs constant supervision

A-2. Participation in group activities and projects:

Frequently emerges as a leader	Active participant but seldom a leader	Ready participant	Cooperates minimally; indifferent	Often a disruptive influence

B. Examples of rating by cumulative points.
B-1. Performance on math word problems:
___Used correct formula or procedure
___Defined all terms and symbols
___Inserted correct values into formula
___Computations correct
___Answer expressed in appropriate units
[Rater checks if each requirement met; score equals number of points checked.]
B-2. Evaluation of an oral report:
3 2 1   Organization of ideas
3 2 1   Use of illustrations and examples
3 2 1   Accuracy of information presented
3 2 1   Appropriateness of conclusions
3 2 1   Presentation (manner, diction, etc.)
[Student rated 1-3 on each point; score equals sum of points.]

nated set of standards. For example, handwriting quality can be rated by comparing a sample of the student's handwriting to a standard set of handwriting samples. These ratings are called *standard scale* ratings.

Other frequently used rating methods—such as forced-choice ratings and graphic rating scales[2]—are of minimal use when rating achievement but may be useful when rating other aspects of class-

---

[2] For more detailed discussion of ratings see Guilford, 1954, Chapter 11, and Kerlinger, 1965, Chapter 28.

room behavior. For example, the *graphic rating scales* can be adapted to measuring approaches to learning or social behavior (see Figure 8.1–A).

Rating scales are relatively easy to construct, apply, and interpret. However, as scores are derived from the observer's judgments rather than directly from student responses, to the extent that the rater makes inferences about the behavior being rated rather than just describing performance, a rating will be less objective than a test score. Like tests, ratings should be standardized, objective, and reliable and measure relevant and important aspects of behavior or performance. If a rating is objective and reliable, an observer will assign the same rating (to the same behavior) on two occasions, and/or different raters will assign the same score (to the same performance).

One requirement for valid ratings is that the behavior being rated be clearly and precisely specified. Often this can best be accomplished by breaking a larger performance down into component tasks, then summing the component scores to obtain an overall rating. Thus, for example, rather than just assigning an overall rating (grade) to an orally presented report, we might rate separate components such as coverage of relevant material, logical organization, drawing correct inferences from the data, clarity of presentation, and ability to answer other students' questions on the topic.

Another requirement is that a sufficiently large sample of behaviors be observed and rated, rather than relying on a few isolated and perhaps atypical performances. In education this will generally be accomplished by *time sampling*—by rating students' performance at various times during the term—rather than intensively sampling at one time. Wide sampling, of course, is designed to insure content validity.

There are a number of errors that plague all types of rating scales. Perhaps the most common is the *halo effect,* the tendency to rate specific aspects of a person's behavior in terms of our general impression of him. Even when they recognize this possibility, raters often commit a *logical error* and rate a person similarly on behaviors that they think should be related. Raters also make the error of central tendency; that is, they tend to overuse middle categories and avoid extreme categories. In contrast, there also are *errors of leniency and severity;* some raters are very lenient in their ratings, while others are very stringent.

To summarize, regardless of their several deficiencies, rating scales are used as the basis for assigning many grades. The teacher, therefore, should take pains to make her ratings as objective as possible and be aware of the common rating errors.

Derived Scores

In education, we generally measure relative achievement; that is, we compare the performance of each student to that of other students, particularly his most immediate competitors, his classmates. Thus test scores and ratings are usually converted to derived or transformed scores, the most common transformations being to percentile ranks or standard scores.

As noted above (see Chapter 3), a percentile rank indicates the student's relative position (ranking) in a norm group, expressed in percentage terms. Therefore, to compute percentile ranks we determine how many persons score below a particular score, convert this number to a proportion, and thence to the percentile scale. This procedure is illustrated in Exhibit 8.1. We see from Exhibit 8.1, for example, that a score of 16 correct corresponds to a percentile rank of 75; stated differently, a student who answered 16 items correctly scored higher than 75 percent of the class members.

Although percentile ranks qua ranks provide a basis for interpreting performance, they are also an intermediate step whenever grades will be assigned to designated proportions of students. Suppose, for example, that we wanted to assign A's to the top 10 percent of the students, B's to the next 15 percent, C's to the middle 50 percent, D's to the next 15 percent and F's to the lowest 10 percent. From Exhibit 8.1 we can see that the minimum score needed to attain an A, B, C and D will be 18, 16, 12, and 10 respectively:

Grade	Desired %	Score	N	Actual %
A	10	18–20	5	12
B	15	16–17	7	18
C	50	12–15	21	52
D	15	10–11	5	12
F	10	0–9	2	5

Of course, any score distribution will not produce the exact grade distribution desired, but we generally can make a close approximation.

Percentile ranks present problems when combining scores on various tests (for example, combining scores on various tests and

EXHIBIT 8.1
COMPUTATION OF PERCENTILE RANKS

To compute percentile ranks for a set of test scores requires the following steps:

1. Develop a frequency distribution. In this example we have used the data from the example in Chapter 5, Exhibit 5.1.
2. Find the number of people scoring lower than each score. This is the cumulative frequency to the lower limit of the score interval (cf_{ll}). For example, the number of persons scoring below 12 is the number scoring from 8 through 11 or $1 + 1 + 2 + 3 = 7$.
3. To correct for using a discrete scale (i.e., we recorded scores only in whole numbers) we add one half of the number of scores in the score interval (n_i) to cf_{ll} to give us a corrected value, the cumulative frequency to the midpoint of the score interval (cf_{mp}). For a score of 12: $cf_{mp} + .5n_i = 7 + .5(4) = 9.0$
4. These values are next converted to cumulative proportions (cp) by dividing cf_{mp} by the number of students in the group —in this example, 40.
5. Cumulative proportions are then converted to percentile ranks by multiplying by 100.

X	(1) f	(2) cf_{ll}	(3) cf_{mp}	(4) cp	(5) P.R.
20	1	39	39.5	.988	99
19	2	37	38.0	.950	95
18	2	35	36.0	.900	90
17	3	32	33.5	.838	84
16	4	28	30.0	.750	75
15	5	23	25.5	.638	64
14	7	16	19.5	.488	49
13	5	11	13.5	.438	44
12	4	7	9.0	.225	22
11	3	4	5.5	.138	14
10	2	2	3.0	.075	8
9	1	1	1.5	.038	4
8	1	0	0.5	.012	1
	40				

Note: There are a number of alternative procedures for computing percentile ranks. For details see a statistics or measurement text.

assignments in order to assign a grade), as the scale units are unequal in size. To legitimately combine scores, all scores must be on the same scale, one having equal-sized units. In education and psychology, the most widely used system is the *standard score* scale, which expresses scores as a deviation from the mean calibrated in standard deviation units (see formula 3.1). Like percentile ranks, standard scores can be used to interpret performance on a single test or assignment; however, their greatest use will be in deriving composite scores (see below). The computation of standard scores is illustrated in Exhibit 8.2.

We now have three ways of expressing performance on a given test or assignment—raw scores, percentile ranks, and standard scores. With the exception of our illustration of converting percentile ranks to grades, we have not discussed changing these scores into grades. As the process of assigning grades to a single test or assignment is analogous to assigning grades to a composite measure, we will delay our discussion of assigning grades until after we have discussed grading systems and methods of combining scores to obtain a composite index of performance.

COURSE MARKS

Assigning students a mark or grade in each course is an almost universal practice, yet one which has also been roundly criticized. In fact, some people have suggested eliminating marks entirely. Ebel (1965) in considering these criticisms suggests that, as marks serve necessary functions, the solution lies not in deemphasizing marks but in improving marking systems so that marks more accurately reflect students' achievements. In particular, he cites the need for (1) clearly defined and generally accepted definitions of what various marks mean, and (2) basing marks on sufficient, relevant, reliable, and objective evidence.

Marking Systems

If a course grade is to have meaning, the bases on which it is assigned and the scale used must be clearly specified. To know that a grade of B represents "above average performance" is not enough; we need to know what performances or skills are reflected by the grade and how the category "above average" is defined.

EXHIBIT 8.2

COMPUTATION OF STANDARD SCORES

The procedure followed in calculating standard scores is illustrated below, using data from our previous example (Exhibits 5.1 and 8.1).

1. Express each score in terms of its deviation from the mean ($x = X - \bar{X}$). In Chapter 5 we found the mean for this set of scores to be 14.1 points; thus, for a score of 12: $x = 12 - 14.1 = -2.1$.
2. Divide each deviation score by the standard deviation: $z = x/s$. As the standard deviation was 2.8 points, for a score of 12:

$$z = -2.1/2.8 = -.75$$

or 12 is .75 standard deviations below the mean.

3. To eliminate decimals and negative numbers, z scores are usually converted to another scale by multiplying by a constant and adding a constant. This transformation changes the mean and standard deviation of the score distributions but does not affect the relationship among scores on their interpretation. In our example we will convert to a scale using a mean of 50 and a standard deviation of 10, or $Z = 50 + 10\ z$. Thus for a score of 12: $Z = 50 + 10\ (-.75) = 42$.

X	(1) x	(2) z	(3) Z
20	5.9	2.11	71
19	4.9	1.75	68
18	3.9	1.39	64
17	2.9	1.04	60
16	1.9	.68	57
15	0.9	.32	53
14	−0.1	−.04	50
13	−1.1	−.39	46
12	−2.1	−.75	42
11	−3.1	−1.11	39
10	−4.1	−1.46	35
9	−5.1	−1.82	32
8	−6.1	−2.18	28

One possibility is to assign a grade of 100 percent to a student who knows all the relevant information about a field and 0 percent to a student who knows nothing about a field. In practice, this generally means assigning a student a grade somewhere between 0 percent and 100 percent, depending upon the student's performance on tests over the course material and/or other assignments. This procedure assumes that the relevant content/skill domain can be completely and precisely defined, that the tests validly sample this domain, and that each individual's score is an accurate indication of his knowledge of the domain. As each individual is compared to a content standard rather than to his peers, each individual's score is independent of all other scores, and we presumably have an *"absolute"* scale.

The reader should see some obvious weaknesses in this grading procedure. As it is virtually impossible to circumscribe the domain and infeasible to test over all possible items, a score of 100 percent has no meaning in any absolute sense. Similarly, a score of 0 percent means only that the student could not answer any items correctly, not that he knows nothing about the field. Consequently, any score between 0 percent and 100 percent is also suspect. Furthermore, how does one determine that 70 percent (or any other arbitrary score) represents minimally acceptable performance?

For these reasons, most schools have shifted to *comparative* or *normative systems*. The most common grading system is probably the 5-step A to F scale, or some variation thereof. In this system, students are ranked in terms of relative achievement, and grades are assigned accordingly.

One question in normative grading concerns the distribution of grades among various categories—how many A's, B's, etc., should be awarded? One frequent suggestion is that grading should be "on the curve," with few extreme grades (A's and F's), slightly more above and below average grades (B's and D's), and the largest number of grades indicating average performance (C's). This approach assumes that achievement will be normally distributed; a tenuous assumption in any but large and unselected samples. Even in a system where the grade distribution over all classes is normal, most classes will be atypical; hence grades in any particular class probably should not be distributed normally.

Another criticism of comparative grading systems is that they allow the student, not the teacher, to set achievement standards. That is, the same percentage of A's would be given if all students worked hard or if all took it easy. Although this argument may have some validity in the abstract, it is doubtful that students will relax in any situation where intraindividual grading is utilized.

Other persons advocate grading students not in comparison to an absolute standard or to their peers but rather by *intraindividual comparisons*. The most frequent suggestions are that students should be graded in relation to their ability or in terms of the amount of improvement shown. After all, if students have different intellectual abilities, is it not fair that they be graded accordingly? Otherwise, less gifted students will always receive lower grades. Grading on improvement ensures that we will reward students on the basis of what they have learned, not knowledge obtained outside the class. And, if developing intrinsic motivation and self-respect are important goals, these can best be accomplished by intraindividual grading.

There is a certain seductiveness to these arguments; but, unfortunately, there are also some problems with intraindividual grading. Grading according to ability assumes that abilities can be precisely measured and that the sole factor determining achievement is academic ability—both tenuous assumptions. Rewarding improvement, of course, gives an advantage to students who start with the least knowledge, as they have the most room to improve. Both procedures utilize differences between scores, thus potentially introducing large amounts of unreliability of measurement. On a somewhat different level, one could argue that most important comparisons, both in education and in the "real world," are interindividual; thus, grades should measure relative achievement.

A final possibility is that performance be reported, not in terms of grades or comparisons, but as *descriptive statements* (see, e.g., Marshall, 1968). These descriptions might be standardized, using a graphic rating scale as the base, or open-ended, with each teacher free to make whatever comments seemed appropriate (for example, a teacher might remark that a student "possesses a large fund of knowledge but does not appear to be able to evaluate or synthesize it."). The presumed advantages of descriptive grading are the avoidance of many of the negative aspects of evaluative grading and that descriptions communicate more information than does a series of symbols. Disadvantages include lack of comparability across courses and the fact that neither relative achievement nor degree of mastery is communicated by such comments.

What this discussion reduces to is that grades, as typically used, are based on implicit teacher-defined standards rather than on an "absolute" content standard or an esoteric statistical theory. Regardless of who defines the standard, the important requirement is that the procedures and scale used be clearly specified, so that grades can be objectively assigned and their meaning unambiguously interpreted.

Course marks are usually based on more than one piece of evidence, with scores on various tests and assignments being combined to obtain an overall grade. When combining scores to determine grades, three questions are paramount: What performances should grades be based on? What relative weight should be given to each component? and, Can component scores be combined to obtain the desired composite?

What information should be included when determining grades? Here, as with most aspects of grading, there is no single answer. Some teachers, particularly at higher educational levels, base grades only on examination scores and specific assignments, such as term papers. Where there is more interaction between teacher and student, as in elementary grades, day-to-day classroom performance will probably weigh heavily. In science courses, laboratory work may be included. In short, the teacher must decide what will be included, taking into account the nature of the subject matter and her teaching philosophy.

There are, however, several guidelines that can be used when deciding whether a particular piece of information should be used to determine grades. (1) Any performance—test, written assignment, etc.—that is included should measure an important skill, one that is relevant to the goals of the particular class. (2) Whenever feasible various types of performances should be used; grades should not be based on only one type of skill—e.g., ability to answer multiple-choice items. (3) Any score used should be objective, be reliable, and measure demonstrated achievement rather than irrelevant considerations, such as the student's attitude or effort. (4) The student should know, in advance, which assignments will be included when determining his grade.

What relative weight should each assignment receive? Again, the answer ultimately reduces to a judgment by the teacher, but, certainly, weightings should reflect the relative importance of the various educational goals and the time devoted to a topic. Thus a high school chemistry teacher might weight various measures:

```
Unit exams (3, 10% each) ..................30%
Laboratory projects (6, 5% each) ...........30%
Classroom participation ...................10%
Final examination .........................30%
```

Another teacher, of course, might assign different relative emphases.

A frequent question concerns the appropriate weighting of final exams. Many teachers and students would argue that no one examination or assignment, including a final examination, should receive such disproportionate weight that one's course grade is determined primarily by the score received on that particular examination. On the other hand, one can argue equally as well that a final examination, if it is cumulative and comprehensive, indicates the student's achievement level at the end of the course and thus should be heavily weighted, even as much as 50 percent of the course grade.

How can grades be combined? The simplest procedure, assuming scores on each assignment and examination are expressed numerically,[3] is to add up the points on the individual assignments, prepare a distribution of total scores, and assign grades from this distribution. This procedure is far from optimal, as no provision is made for differentially weighting various assignments.

Many teachers attempt to weight scores by assigning each exam or assignment a (maximum) number of points which is proportional to the desired emphasis. To use our previous example, the teacher might assign a total of 300 points to all assignments in the following manner:

```
Unit exam (30%)  . . . . . . . . . . . . . .  90 points (30 points/exam)
Laboratory projects (30%)  . . . . .  90 points (15 points/project)
Class participations (10%)  . . . . .  30 points
Final Examination (30%)  . . . . . .  90 points
                                      _____
                                      300 points maximum
```

Points on each assignment are then summed to obtain a grading distribution.

While this procedure would appear to produce the desired differential weighting, it does not necessarily, because when combining scores to obtain a composite the weight of each element will be a function of the variability of the scores rather than the maximum possible score or the mean score. The greater the variability, the greater the effective weight.

Thus each test or assignment will carry its designated weight only if the variability of scores is taken into account. There are several ways of doing this. (See Davis, 1964; Thorndike and Hagen, 1969; or Wood, 1960, for details.) One method is to divide the scores on each assignment by the standard deviation of the score distribution (or an approximation to it) before combining

---

[3] If scores are not expressed numerically, the teacher's only alternative is to make an intuitive subjective combination of scores.

scores. Another method is to correct the desired weightings, taking into account the observed variability of scores. A third method is to record scores on each assignment as standard scores, then combine the standard scores, weighting each in accordance with the desired emphasis. Although the application of such procedures can be tedious, it will insure each element being weighted as desired.

Even these procedures are overly simplistic, as precise weighting also requires taking into account the intercorrelations between the various components. However, if the various elements making up a grade are positively intercorrelated, as generally they will be, and if a relatively large sample of observations is utilized, the differences between weighted composites and simple sums generally will be slight. Therefore, applying corrections will be unnecessary unless the variability of one component is way out of line; in this case a correction would be desirable.

Assigning Grades

The final step is to convert the grades on individual tests and assignments, or the rankings in the composite distribution, into marks on the marking scale used by the institution.

We have already provided one illustration of how this might be done in our discussion of percentile ranks. Here we ranked the students by their scores, then assigned grades according to predetermined percentages. An analogous procedure is probably used in most situations, the variations being in details rather than in principle—e.g., assigning grades from composites rather than from individual test scores. This procedure, in essence, treats all graded work as if it were part of one overall evaluation (i.e., scores on all assignments were summed). Although this procedure has much to recommend it, it also has one drawback—it does not take into account trends over the term. Thus two students with the same composite score, one who started poorly and then performed consistently better throughout the term, and one who started fast, then faded, would obtain the same mark. The teacher's choice here is to hew consistently to the objective standards or to overrule them in individual cases. If he frequently selects the latter course, he will, of course, be destroying some of the objectivity of the grading procedures.

Some institutions have attempted to develop systems that increase the comparability of grades across instructors or across classes. Although the details of these systems vary, they all depend on some "anchor." That is, the grading distribution for a particular class is determined by a variable independent of performance in that particular class—for example, the students' average academic ability. Thus, a class having a larger proportion of able students would have a higher grade distribution than one composed of less able students. (See Ebel, 1965, for an example of such a system). The object of such procedures is, of course, to increase the comparability and meaningfulness of grades.

SOME PROBLEMS IN GRADING

The reader should have noted that we have only considered grading achievement or performance, not grading effort, classroom deportment, attitudes, or other nonintellectual characteristics. The omission of these areas was deliberate as we feel grades should be indices of students' achievement. This is not to say that other characteristics, behaviors, and attitudes are unimportant; far from it. Rather it means that these other variables should be rated (graded) separately from achievement.

One possible method of reporting nonacademic behaviors or characteristics is by rating scales. Graphic rating scales can be adapted to many of the relevant characteristics and are relatively simple to apply and interpret (see Figure 8.1, above). Another possibility is to discuss these areas in teacher-parent conferences and thereby not make them part of the student's permanent record.

While we have discussed grading as if it were necessary (and, in fact, have concluded that grading is necessary), many people feel that grading is unnecessary or even a detriment to learning. Their position is often stated: "It's not the grade that is important, but what you learn." And a strong argument can be made for this position.[4] However, while it is undoubtedly true that grades often do not reflect what students think is important, this is not the function of grades; grades are indices of students' mastery of basic knowledge and skills. Furthermore, there is an implicit assumption in this position that what students learn and what tests and grades measure are independent. However, if grades are based on well-designed tests and assignments that include performances which

---

[4] One should also note that grades, as typically used, do not indicate what the student has learned, but rather how much he knows at the end of the term.

are both basic to the field and relevant to students' interests, this independence need not occur.

A tempering of this position can be seen in several alternative grading procedures. One is the "pass-fail" system. Although a pass-fail system probably reduces some of the pressures associated with grade getting, it does not completely eliminate them. Furthermore, it substitutes a two-step scale for a more reliable multiple-step scale. (One could argue that grading pressures would be reduced with a scale having a large number of steps, as differences between grades would be less crucial—e.g., is not the difference between a 92 and a 93 less than that between an A and a B?) Another possibility is to use only descriptive comments rather than marks. While having certain advantages, this system generally results in less standardized and hence less meaningful grades and encounters problems when making decisions as to whether students have attained various levels of mastery.

Finally, we might ask if grading is measurement or evaluation. Adopting the procedures advocated in this chapter will result in relatively objective marks which describe students' relative achievement. In this sense, grades will be measurements. But as grades will be interpreted and inferences made from grades, an evaluative connotation cannot be avoided.

SUMMARY

Grades and course marks, although being reported on diverse scales, are generally measures of relative achievement. They serve several purposes, the chief of which are providing feedback to students regarding the effectiveness of their learning and serving as aids to educational and vocational planning.

Grading occurs on two levels—grading individual assignments or examinations and determining course marks. Some of the former are based on test scores and others are performance ratings. In many instances, these scores are made more meaningful by conversion to another type of score, such as percentile ranks. Course marks are based on performance on several tests and assignments; here the major measurement problem is how to optimally combine scores.

Grading systems are based on several different philosophies. Some attempt to compare a student to an "absolute" standard; others are comparative or normative, comparing a student to his peers; still others are intraindividual, comparing a student's achievement to his ability or a previous measure of achievement. In essence, however, most systems reduce to a teacher-defined scale. Thus, besides the requirements of objective scoring or rating, basing grades on sufficient samples of performance, and using reliable measures, one must always clearly specify the procedures used in deriving grades and the meaning of the various categories on the grading scale.

REFERENCES

DAVIS, F. B. *Educational Measurements and Their Interpretation.* Belmont, Calif.: Wadsworth Publishing Co., Inc., 1964.

EBEL, R. L. *Measuring Educational Achievement.* Englewood Cliffs, N.J.: Prentice-Hall, Inc., 1965.

GUILFORD, J. P. *Psychometric Methods.* 2nd ed. New York: McGraw-Hill Book Co., 1954.

KERLINGER, F. N. *Foundations of Behavioral Research.* New York: Holt, Rinehart & Winston, Inc., 1965.

MARSHALL, M. S. *Teaching without Grades.* Corvallis: Oregon State University Press, 1968.

SMITH, A. Z., and DOBBIN, J. E. "Marks and Marking Systems," in C. W. HARRIS (ed.), *Encyclopedia of Educational Research.* 3rd ed., pp. 783–91. New York: The Macmillan Company, 1960.

THORNDIKE, R. L., and HAGEN, E. P. *Measurement and Evaluation in Psychology and Education.* 3rd ed. New York: John Wiley & Sons, Inc., 1969.

WOOD, D. A. *Test Construction.* Columbus, Ohio: Charles E. Merrill Publishing Co., 1960.

9

EVALUATION OF INSTRUCTION

In the previous chapters we have been primarily concerned with testing and evaluating individual students; tests were used to measure students' achievements, skills, abilities, and personality characteristics. Only when discussing item analysis procedures did we make inferences about the quality or effectiveness of the educational process. In this chapter we will look at tests in terms of information they can provide regarding the effectiveness of instruction.

Some examples may clarify our concern. One occasionally reads a newspaper article which states that the scores of students in the local school system were markedly higher than the national average on a standardized achievement battery. Or you may read that a number of graduates of the local high school have been accepted into prestigeful colleges or have won scholarships and awards. Or a study might show that the graduates of a particular university were highly successful in their careers. In each of these examples there is an implicit assumption that the quality of the school was responsible for the results.

Consider several different examples. A study might show that children taught to read by the "look-say" method score lower on a reading test than do students taught phonetically. Or a study might show that there are no differences in achievement when a class is taught by lecture, in discussion sections, or when each student works independently. Another study might show that learning is more efficient when the material is presented by teaching machines than when presented by teachers and textbooks. Or, a department chairman may note that Mr. White's classes consistently score higher than Mr. Green's classes on the departmental exam. In these examples there is an implication that a particular teaching method, curriculum, or teacher is more effective than another method, curriculum, or teacher.

In a more general sense, each study evaluated some aspect of instruction. Some were designed specifically to evaluate instruction; others used *ad hoc* or fortuitous collections of data. In either case, however, we went beyond merely measuring educational outcomes; we evaluated the instruction.

Purposes of Evaluation

The purposes of evaluating instruction are to make judgments and decisions about instruction and instructional programs (Wittrock, 1969), and to produce information that can be used in educational decision making (Astin & Panos, in press). The decision may be to continue or terminate a particular program, to modify present practices, to adopt a new program, or to develop a different program.

An evaluation may focus on the process or the outcome of an educational program. That is, we may be interested in what students know or can do at the end of instruction (outcomes) or we may be more concerned with evaluating the processes that produce these outcomes. More specifically, Wittrock (1969) has distinguished between : (1) the evaluation of learners—studies of students' achievement and performance; (2) the evaluation of educational environments—characteristics of the curriculum and the physical and human characteristics of the school environment; (3) the evaluation of learning—the study of what student behaviors have changed as a result of instruction; and (4) the evaluation of instruction—the study of the interaction of student characteristics and the educational environment and their effects on learning.

In addition, we can evaluate immediate outcomes (what the student knows at the end of a course) or longer range outcomes (retention and transfer to other courses and areas). The majority of the studies reported in the literature have used immediate outcomes and, in Wittrock's classification, have been studies of learners. This should not be surprising, as other types of evaluations are more time-consuming, expensive, and complex.

METHODS OF EVALUATING INSTRUCTION

In order to evaluate instruction two conditions must be present: a specified set of instructional objectives, and at least two alternative methods of attaining these objectives (Astin & Panos, in press). Unless we can specify the objectives we are attempting to attain, we have no basis for determining whether they have been attained or evaluating the effectiveness of the educational program. The need for alternative methods of attaining these objectives may not be so apparent. Although at times we evaluate methods individually—as when a teacher judges the quality of a particular book or curriculum—any true evaluation requires that a given program be compared to other alternatives (including the alternative of doing nothing).

Furthermore, whenever we do an evaluation, we assume that there is a causal relationship between some aspect of the instructional program and the outcome. For example, if we compare two methods of teaching history and find that one method results in higher achievement, we imply that some variable (that differs between the two methods) is the causal agent that produces the differential achievement. However, because many studies in education, including those evaluating instruction, do not allow control of all relevant variables, making causal inferences is quite difficult (see below).

Types of Studies

The information used as a basis for an evaluation can come from many sources. Frequently anecdotal reports or fortuitously collected information are used as the basis for decision making. Examples would include using available achievement test scores to evaluate an instructional program, using students' comments to evaluate instructors, or relying on a teacher's experience in using a particular technique or materials. The distinguishing feature of this approach is that data, often collected for some other purpose, are used, *post hoc,* to make an evaluation. These data are obviously of limited usefulness because of their selective and incidental quality.

Other evaluations are based on more formal, yet subjective, judgments. For example, teachers may evaluate a textbook, curriculum, or instructional method by systematically studying the content, procedures, and goals of the program. Here, in contrast to the previous approach, the objectives and goals are clearly specified, and the program is compared to these objectives; however, quantitative data are not collected.

Descriptive studies collect objective data to answer specified questions. For example, a scholastic aptitude test might be administered to students in a particular school to ascertain their level of intellectual ability; scores on an achievement battery might be used to determine students' relative ability to do arithmetic manipulations and arithmetic reasoning; or the grades assigned by various instructors might be studied to determine if they graded differently. Most empirical studies used in educational decision making are descriptive in nature. Although, logically, these studies do not allow causal inferences to be made, in practice causal relations are generally assumed; that is, if we find one group of students has higher scores on both a scholastic aptitude and an achievement test, we assume their high ability produced their good achievement.

The best basis for evaluations of instruction would be the results of experiments where students were randomly assigned to various treatment conditions (e.g., instructional methods) and their learning measured. Such "pure" experiments are relatively uncommon in education because the exigencies of the educational setting do not allow for random assignment of students to instructional methods or for control of all relevant variables or true replication. Thus most educational studies are *quasi-experiments,* studies that allow manipulation of treatment conditions but not random assignments of students to treatments (Campbell and Stanley, 1963). These quasi experiments do, however, allow certain types of causal inferences to be made.

Classes of Variables

Any study evaluating instruction must include measures of three classes of variables: inputs, outputs, and treatments or operations (Astin & Panos, in press).

The *inputs* are the characteristics that students bring to the learning situation—their knowledge, skills, abilities, aptitudes, interests, attitudes, values, and so on.[1] Input characteristics influence both output and the educational environment. To illustrate the latter, suppose that a given educational program is relatively ineffective and thus has produced few changes in students. In this situation, differences at the end of the instruction (the output) will mainly reflect individual differences in input; those students who had the most knowledge of the subject at the beginning of the course will also have the most at its termination. Input characteristics may also influence the educational environment. For example, a class composed of students who are highly motivated and achievement oriented will be different from one where students have little academic motivation, regardless of the teaching method or curriculum used.

Outputs refer to the students' knowledge, achievements, skills, attitudes, abilities, etc., at the completion of instruction. More particularly, they are measures of those characteristics which are particularly relevant, i.e., that reflect the goals of the instructional process. That is, they are the criterion measures. Usually, but not necessarily, these are measures of relative achievement in attaining the immediate goals of instruction.

Although we usually think of *treatments* in terms of variables that directly and obviously influence learning—e.g., curricular methods and emphases, teaching methods, class size, characteristics of the teacher—this category properly includes other variables —e.g., the social context of the learning situation, characteristics of the students, the campus "climate." In short, any variable that distinguishes a particular learning environment or treatment must be considered as a possible causal agent.

The possible relationships between these three classes of variables are shown in Figure 9.1. Note that we might choose to study only one class of variables or an interaction between classes. For example, we might study how the characteristics of its students influence a college's climate or environment (relation A), differential achievement under two teaching methods (relation B), or what sort of students succeed in a given curriculum (relation C). However, the most useful and important studies are those that consider the joint impact of input characteristics and treatments on outputs, the class that Wittrock calls evaluation of instruction.

---

[1] Notice the correspondence between these variables and the questions raised in Chapter 1; for example, input measures are designed to answer our first question concerning the level of abilities, skills, and personality characteristics.

FIGURE 9.1

RELATIONSHIPS BETWEEN CLASSES OF VARIABLES IN EVALUATION STUDIES

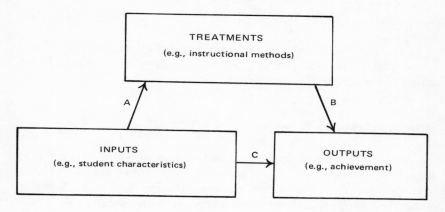

Source: Based on A. W. Astin & R. J. Panos, "The Evaluation of Educational Research." In R. L. Thorndike, Editor, *Educational Measurement,* Second Edition, American Council on Education, 1970.

Steps in an Evaluation Study

How might one conduct an evaluation study? Although every study will have to be designed individually, taking into account its peculiar requirements, a sequence of steps to be followed in most studies can be identified:

1. Specify the goals of the instructional program, the desired outcomes, and the alternative procedures for attaining these outcomes.

2. Select a sample of students to be used in the evaluation study. These students should be representative of the students for whom the program is designed. For example, a beginning reading program should be evaluated using a sample of first-grade students.

3. Measure students' standing on relevant characteristics—e.g., their present level of achievement, learning skills and attitudes, personality characteristics. These are the input variables.

4. Apply the instructional program (treatment) to the sample. In most studies, only a portion of the sample will receive each treatment—for example, half of the students may be taught by lectures, the other half in small discussion sections.

5. Monitor the effects of the treatment. Although we may only measure achievement at the end of instruction, if we constantly monitor performance, we can better determine when and how learning occurs.

6. Analyze the results and draw conclusions; this is the evaluation phase.

7. Put the results into practice by modifying present procedures or adopting the new method. At this point we essentially begin anew and evaluate the new procedure.

Problems in Evaluating Instruction

Although the procedures outlined in the previous section may appear straightforward, there are numerous problems in any evaluation study. This is not the place to discuss these problems in detail, but brief consideration of some common problems may give a better understanding of the complexity of the evaluation process.[2]

Many of the problems in evaluating instruction are basically problems of experimental design. Perhaps the major one is the inability to assign students randomly to treatment conditions. When students are not randomly assigned to conditions, there is an increased probability of interactions between student characteristics and educational environments which, in turn, may affect the outcomes. A clear example is furnished by studies comparing the effectiveness of several colleges or curricula in producing changes in students. As students who enter various colleges and curricula differ in abilities, motivation, interests, and personality characteristics, any observed changes in students may be a function of the type of students who enter the curricula, the different educational environments (i.e., treatments), or the interaction of the two forces. Even if students could be randomly assigned, not every possible relevant student characteristic will be measured, leaving open the possibility that some unmeasured factor is the primary causal agent.

Second, it is often difficult to specify exactly what the effective treatment conditions are, or even to identify all environmental effects. Even when we systematically describe the environment, it

---

[2] For more detailed discussion of the process and problems of evaluating instruction, see Astin & Panos, in press; Campbell & Stanley, 1963; Cronbach, 1963, 1967; Gage, 1963; Gagné, 1967; Kerlinger, 1965; Tyler, 1951; Wittrock, 1969; Wittrock & Wiley, in press.

is usually in qualitative rather than quantitative terms. Furthermore, there are numerous interactions among environmental conditions. For example, with the possible exception of methods using automated devices (e.g., computers) to present content materials, it is usually difficult to separate the influences of the teacher from those attributable to the teaching method or the curricular materials. Each teacher will probably be more familiar with, have more faith in, be better prepared to teach, or otherwise do a better job with one particular method or set of materials, thus producing an interaction between teacher, method, and materials.

Third, a test (or any other procedure used to measure learning) may not be equally valid for evaluating different types of outcomes. For example, a history test emphasizing the identification of names and dates would give an advantage to students who had taken a course that stressed persons and sequences of historical events over students taught by a method emphasizing causes underlying historical trends and events. However, as Cronbach (1963) has pointed out, such tests can be valuable in measuring the amount of transfer and incidental learning.

Fourth, using grouped data may mask student-method interactions. For example, two teaching methods may result in the same average per-pupil gain in achievement; however, under one method the brighter students may make large gains and average and below average students may show no gain, while the other method might produce smaller gains, but for all students.

Fifth, students may learn more, not because of the effectiveness of the method, but because of the increased motivation which comes from taking part in a novel or experimental program. For example, a study may show that using a computer for mathematics drill may increase computational skills more than other teaching methods. However, this better performance may not be directly attributable to the content of the method, but rather to the added motivation which results from the novelty of using the computer. This phenomenon is the well-known "Hawthorne effect."

Sixth, usually it is infeasible, in terms of time or money, to determine the long-term effects of instructional programs. Thus most evaluation studies consider only relatively immediate outcomes. Yet it is possible that a method producing a lesser immediate change may result in larger long-range gains or transfer to a wider variety of situations.

Finally, as most educational instructions operate within a limited budget, one must also consider the utility of any program—the costs and benefits associated with any instructional method.

Even if a study shows that students learn to read more efficiently using a computer-based reading program, this knowledge will be of little value if the school system does not have the financial resources to buy the necessary computer time.

EXAMPLES OF EVALUATION STUDIES

In the previous section we discussed several methods of evaluating instruction; in this section we will present illustrations of evaluation studies. These will be categorized using Wittrock's classification scheme.

Evaluation of Learners

Studies evaluating learners focus on the behavior and characteristics of students and on individual differences among students. Most commonly they are studies of output variables. For example, a college or high school might study its attrition rate; scores on standardized tests may be used to measure students' achievement; or the average starting salary, or percent of students attending graduate school, may be used as an index of the effectiveness of an undergraduate program.

An example of a more comprehensive study using this approach is the National Assessment of Educational Progress (Committee on Assessing the Progress of Education, 1968; Tyler, Merwin, and Ebel, 1966). The project will develop and administer tests assessing achievement in 10 areas[3] to a national sample of children and adults. The primary purpose of the Assessment is to obtain information on the average achievement at different ages; thus testing will be at four age levels—age 9, after children have been exposed to the basic education program; age 13, following completion of elementary school; 17, the last age at which most students are in school; and young adults, aged 26–35. Results will also be reported by sex, four geographic regions, type of community, race, and socioeconomic level.

Output studies do not directly identify causal agents, as the relationships between treatment (environmental) conditions and outcomes are not studied. However, they do require specification

---

[3] The 10 areas to be covered by the National Assessment include: literature, science, social studies, writing, citizenship, music, mathematics, reading, art, and vocational education.

of the desired educational outcomes and development of measures of these outcomes, both desirable exercises. In addition, they can provide baseline data against which outcomes of other programs can be compared.

We can also study inputs, the characteristics and behaviors of students entering an educational program. The most frequent data are scores on standardized aptitude and achievement tests, records of past academic performance, and biographical variables. Here again, although causal relations are not studied, an understanding of the nature of the student body may provide a basis for designing or modifying educational programs or for the placement of students in appropriate courses and programs. Examples of input studies are the two national college admissions testing programs, the College Entrance Examination Board and the American College Testing Program; both programs provide summary descriptions (class profiles) of the achievements, abilities, goals, plans, and other characteristics of their entering freshman class to colleges using their testing program.

Evaluation of Environments

Most evaluations of educational environments are systematic, qualitative descriptions of some aspect of an educational program. For example, an instructor may study various textbooks to see which ones best meet the objectives that he has set for his class; an administrator or curriculum specialist may evaluate a course by studying its goals, assignments, source materials, tests, projects, and so on; or an educational program may be evaluated by comparison to a set of standards, as when a school is accredited by a regional accreditation agency or as in Conant's studies of American schools (see e.g., Conant, 1959).[4]

Quantitative descriptions of educational environments have also been developed. For example, Pace has developed an instrument, the College and University Environment Scales (CUES), which measures the "climate" of a college as perceived by the students attending the college (Pace, 1963). And Astin and his co-workers have developed several procedures for describing college environments, all based on the characteristics and behaviors of the students attending various colleges (see, e.g., Astin, 1965, 1968[A]).

---

[4] Notice that the judgmental process used to evaluate curricular methods or materials is very similar to the process of determining content validity.

Studies evaluating learning focus on changes in students, therefore they require two measures: a pretest (administered at the beginning of instruction or at a given point of time) and a posttest (administered at the completion of instruction or at a subsequent time). The difference between the two performances (posttest score minus pretest score) is the measure of change, a measure of the amount learned.

As education is concerned with producing changes in students, one might expect that such studies would be commonplace. Although we may look at students' year-to-year scores on achievement batteries to obtain an indication of their development or growth, formal studies are relatively rare. There are several possible reasons for the dearth of such studies. These studies, while indicating if change has occurred, do not identify the factors producing change; thus they are of little value in improving or modifying instructional programs. In addition, systematic pretesting usually does not occur; we either assume that the student has mastered the material taught in the previous course or, if the courses are not sequential, that he knows nothing about the subject.

The pretest-posttest paradigm has been used to study changes on variables other than achievement in academic subjects. For example, there have been a number of studies of changes in college students' attitudes, values, and personality characteristics as the result of college experience (see, e.g., Sanford, 1956, 1962; Katz, 1968).

Evaluation of Instruction

Studies classified in this category utilize all three classes of measures—inputs, outputs, and treatments. As both pretest and posttest measures are available, what and how much has been learned can be determined. As environmental (treatment) conditions have been specified and manipulated, causal relations can be established and those aspects of the treatment which produced the change identified.

An example has been provided by Cronbach (1967) in an illustration of how different instructional methods can be related to individual differences between learners. Suppose that a given course is taught by two different methods, that several student characteristics are measured prior to the course, that students are randomly assigned to methods, and that a measure of achievement is collected at the end of the course. After the achievement data (output) are collected, student characteristics (input) are correlated with achievement, and the relationship is plotted graphically. We obtain the results shown in Figure 9.2. This figure shows that students with higher input (pretest) scores achieve better under Method A while those with lower pretest scores have higher achievement under Method B. In other words, an interaction of student characteristics with teaching methods determines the level of achievement. These results can then be used to assign students to teaching methods so as to maximize achievement.

Another example is provided by Astin's (1968[B]) attempt to determine whether differences in achievement between college seniors (as measured by Graduate Record Examination area tests) can be attributed to the quality of the college the student attended. Although graduates of different colleges do, in fact, obtain different average scores on these tests, Astin argued that these results might reflect the characteristics of the students attending the various colleges rather than differences in the quality of their educational programs. Thus he analyzed the relationships between numerous college characteristics and achievement, taking into account the characteristics of students attending various colleges. He found that the influence of the college was negligible and that differences in achievement were primarily a function of the characteristics of students who entered different colleges.

A third example is Glaser's (1968) description of an individualized program for teaching mathematics in elementary school. The program included detailed specification of the objectives of the curriculum, designing a sequence of instructional units that paralleled these objectives, pretesting students at the beginning of each unit, continuous monitoring of performance as students progressed through each unit, and testing for mastery. This program not only contains all the elements necessary for evaluating instruction but also provides cumulative records of each student's progress (see Figure 9.3) and allows feedback on progress to be used in adapting instruction to the individual student.

As was noted above, most educational settings do not allow random assignment of students to treatments and thus do not allow for true experimental evaluation. In these situations, we often study relationships between treatments and outcomes. An

FIGURE 9.2
AN EXAMPLE OF A STUDY EVALUATING INSTRUCTION

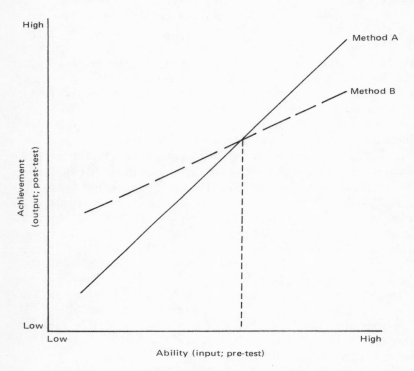

Note: Graph shows relation of ability to achievement under two teaching methods. Students whose ability scores fall to the right of the dotted line would be assigned to Method A; those scoring to the left would be assigned to Method B.

Source: Adapted from L. J. Cronbach, "How Can Instruction Be Adapted to Individual Differences?" in R. M. Gagné (ed.), *Learning and Individual Differences* (Columbus, Ohio: Charles E. Merrill Publishing Co., 1967), pp. 32–33.

example is the *International Study of Achievement in Mathematics* (Husén, 1967), in which mathematics achievement was studied by using a common test in 12 countries. Characteristics of the schools and countries were related to achievement, and inferences were drawn as to which factors were associated with differential achievement. Another example, using similar methods, is the United States Office of Education's study *Equality of Educational Opportunity* (Coleman, *et al.*, 1966).

FIGURE 9.3

A CUMULATIVE RECORD OF A STUDENT'S PROGRESS IN MATHEMATICS

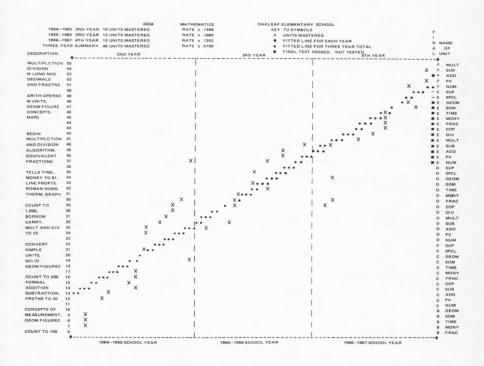

Source: Robert Glaser. "Adapting the Elementary School Curriculum to Individual Performance," Figure 6, page 24. From *Proceedings of the 1967 Invitational Conference on Testing Programs.* Princeton, N.J., Educational Testing Service, © 1968. Reprinted with permission of author and publisher.

THE ROLE OF TESTS IN EVALUATION

It should be obvious that tests play an essential role in the evaluation of instruction being used as measures of each of the three classes of variables: inputs, outputs, and environments (treatments).

Because testing and evaluation are so intertwined, many people tend to equate the two processes; however, they do differ. Tests are only one possible type of measure, albeit often the most efficient and objective method of obtaining data. Other sources are also used—e.g., reactions of learners; judgments by teachers, administrators, or curriculum experts; and measures of time and costs. But the fundamental distinction relates to the goals of the two processes. Tests provide an objective index, a measurement of student performance or environmental characteristics. Evaluation, by definition, implies that an estimate of value or worth is placed on that measurement. Although evaluative elements are built into all testing procedures (for example, we only measure "important" outcomes), testing is basically objective and nonjudgmental. The evaluative aspect enters when interpreting test scores.

Note also that evaluation may require different standards for tests. Most test construction procedures are designed for tests which measure individual differences. But, in evaluation studies, items which do not discriminate between individuals will be included on the test if they measure important outcomes. That is, the primary criterion for item selection is that the items sample important concepts (content validity) rather than discriminate between individuals. Furthermore, in evaluating instruction we are generally more interested in group differences than individual scores; thus a test which is too unreliable for individual use may be sufficiently stable for measuring group trends.[5]

SUMMARY

In this chapter we have focused on the evaluation of instructional methods and materials, in distinction to the measurement and evaluation of individual differences. The main purposes of evaluation studies were seen as to improve instruction and to aid in educational decision making.

[5] Group averages, being based on a larger number of observations than individual scores, are thus more stable.

Four types of evaluation studies were discussed and illustrated: (1) studies of the characteristics of students—called the evaluation of learners; (2) studies of educational environments, methods, and materials—evaluation of environments; (3) studies which focus on changes in students—evaluation of learning; and (4) studies of the interaction of learners and treatment conditions in determining achievement—evaluation of instruction.

It was pointed out that tests are used as measures of each of the three relevant classes of variables: input measures, output measures, and treatment conditions (environments). However, it was also emphasized that testing and evaluation are separate processes and that tests used in evaluation studies must meet different standards than tests used to measure individual differences.

REFERENCES

ASTIN, A. W. *Who Goes Where to College?* Chicago: Science Research Associates, Inc., 1965.

ASTIN, A. W. *The College Environment.* Washington, D.C.: American Council on Education, 1968 (A).

ASTIN, A. W., "Undergraduate Achievement and Institutional 'Excellence,'" *Science,* Vol. 161 (1968 [B]), pp. 661–68.

ASTIN, A. W., and PANOS, R. J. "The Evaluation of Educational Programs," in R. L. THORNDIKE (ed.), *Educational Measurement.* Rev. ed. Washington, D.C.: American Council on Education, in press.

CAMPBELL, D. T., and STANLEY, J. C. "Experimental and Quasi-Experimental Designs for Research on Teaching," in N. L. GAGE (ed.), *Handbook of Research on Teaching.* Chicago: Rand McNally & Co., 1963.

COLEMAN, J. S., *et al. Equality of Educational Opportunity.* Washington, D.C.: U.S. Department of Health, Education, and Welfare, 1966.

COMMITTEE ON ASSESSING THE PROGRESS OF EDUCATION. *How Much Are Students Learning? Plans for a National Assessment of Education.* Ann Arbor, Mich., 1968.

CONANT, J. B. *The American High School Today.* New York: McGraw-Hill Book Company, 1959.

CRONBACH, L. J. "Course Improvement through Evaluation," *Teacher's College Record,* Vol. 64 (1963), pp. 672–83.

CRONBACH, L. J. "How Can Instruction Be Adapted to Individual

Differences?" in R. M. GAGNÉ (ed.), *Learning and Individual Differences*. Columbus, Ohio: Charles E. Merrill Publishing Co., 1967. Pp. 23–39.

GAGE, N. L. (ed.) *Handbook of Research on Teaching*. Chicago: Rand McNally & Co., 1963.

GAGNÉ, R. M. (ed.) *Learning and Individual Differences*. Columbus, Ohio: Charles E. Merrill Publishing Co., 1967.

GLASER, R. "Adapting the Elementary School Curriculum to Individual Performance," *Proceedings of the 1967 Invitational Conference on Testing Problems*, pp. 3–36. Princeton, N.J.: Educational Testing Service, 1968.

HUSÉN, T. (ed.) *International Study of Achievement in Mathematics*. 2 vols. New York: John Wiley & Sons, Inc., 1967.

KATZ, J., and Associates. *No Time for Youth*. San Francisco: Jossey-Bass, Inc., Publishers, 1968.

KERLINGER, F. N. *Foundations of Behavioral Research*. New York: Holt, Rinehart & Winston, Inc., 1965.

PACE, C. R. *College and University Environment Scales: (Preliminary) Technical Manual*. Princeton, N.J.: Educational Testing Service, 1963.

SANFORD, N. (ed.) "Personality Developmental during College Years," *Journal of Social Issues*, Vol. 12 (1956), No. 4.

SANFORD, N. (ed.) *The American College*. New York: John Wiley & Sons, Inc., 1962.

TYLER, R. W. "The Functions of Measurement in Improving Instruction," in E. F. Lindquist (ed.), *Educational Measurement*, pp. 47–67. Washington, D.C.: American Council on Education, 1951.

TYLER, R. W.; MERWIN, J. C., and EBEL, R. L. "Symposium: A National Assessment of Educational Progress," *Journal of Educational Measurement*, Vol. 3 (1966), pp. 1–17.

WITTROCK, M. C. "The Evaluation of Instruction: Cause and Effect Relations in Naturalistic Data." (Evaluation Comment, Center for the Study of Evaluation, University of California, Los Angeles, May, 1969.)

WITTROCK, M. C., and WILEY, D. E. (eds.) *The Evaluation of Instructions: Issues and Problems*. New York: Holt, Rinehart & Winston, Inc., in press.

10

RECAPITULATION

Before closing we will devote several pages to briefly recapitulating some of the major points made throughout the book, pulling some of the seemingly diverse topics together and projecting some trends into the future.

What Is a Test Score?

Most of the important points regarding test scores can be summarized in a few simple propositions. First, a test score is only an estimate, it is not a precise index. This is evident from the discussion of consistency of measurement, where we indicated that each score contained some measurement error, and from the fact that any test contains only a sample of all possible items. Thus test scores should be interpreted as ranges or bands, rather than as absolute, immutable indices.

Second, a test measures current status; it indicates the student's present level of performance, not how he attained this level. To understand why a student obtained a particular score requires extensive knowledge of his past experiences, both within and without the formal educational system. Furthermore, as testing conditions can influence test performance, the circumstances of the testing must also be taken into account when interpreting a score.

Third, a test score must be interpreted with reference to a particular norm group. (An exception is criterion-referenced scores.) Thus, to interpret a student's performance we must have a clear understanding of the composition of the group his performance is being compared to, the norm group. Particularly vital is how each individual student's previous experiences compare to those of the persons comprising the norm group.

Fourth, a test score is meaningless unless there is a foundation of validity evidence undergirding the test. Unless we know what the test measures, we cannot interpret individual scores. On most educational tests the important validity question is whether the test items adequately sample an educationally relevant content or skill domain.

Fifth, a test score is only one possible index of a student's ability. The teacher, obviously, has several other bases for assessing students' performance—e.g., homework assignments, projects, classroom recitation and discussions, papers and reports. But tests are one of the best (if not the best) assessment methods, as they provide more standardized, objective, reliable, and valid estimates than do the other methods.

Sixth, a test score should be a basis for making a decision regarding the progress of a particular student or group of students or the evaluation of an instructional program or method. Thus, unless test scores provide useful information, the time devoted to administering and scoring the test has been wasted. In other words, tests should be used only when the results will contribute to the improvement of some aspect of the educational process.

The Model

In Chapter 1 we outlined an approach to test usage in educational settings. Later we made little explicit reference to the model. We might now review how the material discussed in subsequent chapters fits the model.

Much of the testing done in education is designed (but not necessarily used) to determine students' present level of developed abilities so as to help plan subsequent educational experiences. Tests of aptitudes and personality characteristics fall in this category. Scores on standardized achievement batteries and past grades also serve this function, as they indicate which aspects of the curriculum students have mastered. But, as was mentioned earlier, systematic evidence relating student characteristics to optimal educational programming is usually lacking.

In most settings there is some monitoring of student progress. The administration of chapter or unit examinations, either teacher-made or those supplied with the textbook, is an almost universal practice. In addition, monitoring may be accomplished by homework, classroom recitation and discussion, and other assignments. Standardized tests are seldom used for monitoring progress, except for reading tests used in the elementary grades. Computer-assisted instruction and programmed learning systems can, of course, provide almost continual monitoring and feedback to the student.

Like end-of-unit examinations, course or semester examinations are almost universal. With the exception of schools which utilize departmental examinations, these are usually teacher-built examinations. Although standardized tests covering the content of specific courses have been developed, these are most often used in courses following new approaches (the newer mathematics and science curricula) or to evaluate atypical educational experiences (e.g., the College Level Examination Program can be used to award credit for independent study).

The usual method for measuring transfer, integration, and long-term retention is the standardized achievement battery. At several places we have referred to these tests as yearly achievement batteries, since many schools administer these batteries to all students once a year, particularly during the elementary and junior high years. Usually the purposes of these tests are to measure students' growth and to evaluate the general effectiveness of the school. As the domain covered by each individual test generally is broader than the content of any single course, these tests, in a sense, measure ability to integrate material from various courses.

School Testing Programs

We will not propose an "ideal" school testing program, feeling that any testing program[1] should be tailored to the unique objectives of the particular school. Thus no one prescription will be

---

[1] Although, in the broad sense, a school testing program encompasses all the tests administered in a school, as used here the term refers to the standardized achievement batteries, scholastic aptitude tests, special aptitude tests, and personality measures which are periodically administered to all students within the school or within a particular grade.

applicable in all settings. However, certain guidelines can be abstracted from our previous discussion, ones which will direct the development of the testing program. Among the most important of these are:

1. Tests should be administered only if they will be used. This implies that only those tests that will be used to make decisions about the large majority of students or evaluate the educational program should be routinely administered to all students; that tests utilized in remedial instruction or guidance should be administered on an individual basis; and that tests which may provide interesting data but will not aid educational planning (e.g., most personality measures) can best be forgotten.

2. The frequency of testing should reflect the rate with which skills are developing. When skills are changing rapidly, such as reading ability in the primary grades, we may want to administer a standardized (reading) test several times a year. For most other achievement areas testing once a year, or even every other year, will be sufficient. Measures of mental ability and scholastic aptitude are generally most useful just prior to points of transition, say, from elementary to junior high school. At these points the child may have options between different curricula, and information regarding his abilities may be pertinent to his educational planning.

3. The more specific the information, the more useful it will be. Thus a battery providing scores in several arithmetic areas (e.g., concepts, computations) and several reading areas (e.g., vocabulary, sentence meaning, paragraph meaning) will generally yield more useful information than a battery providing only one arithmetic and one reading score. One must be sure, however, that each score reported is based on enough items to be both a reliable and a valid index of the characteristic measured.

4. The testing program should allow for various interindividual and intraindividual comparisons. Interindividual comparisons will be possible to the extent that (1) the test publisher provides normative data based on groups defined by several relevant characteristics (e.g., sex, grade, geographic region, type of schools and/or community) and (2) local norms are available. The greater the diversity of normative data, the more useful the information. The most important intraindividual comparisons are between performance in various achievement areas and measures of growth from year to year. The former is the major advantage of the battery approach—students' scores in various areas can be com-

pared, as they are based on a common norm group. The latter is possible by using tests which are published with different forms for various age levels.

5. Tests should be chosen with an eye both to the average ability level of the students and the variability among students. Not only should a test be of appropriate difficulty for the average student,[2] it should also have enough "top" or "ceiling" so that the better students can demonstrate the limits of their knowledge, yet contain enough easy items so that it is possible to discriminate between the weaker students.

Trends

Having discussed current approaches to testing in education, we will close by mentioning what appear to be some of the more important emerging trends.

First, there will be numerous attempts to develop tests for areas where previously no acceptable tests were available. The surge of interest in measuring creativity during the past decade provides one such example. Other new areas include attempts to measure complex intellectual abilities and cognitive styles, particularly ones which are central to a theory of intellectual structure. Examples include tests measuring the various dimensions of Guilford's structure-of-the-intellect model and tests derived from Piagetian thinking.

Concurrently, we will see more flexibility in testing formats rather than almost sole reliance on paper-and-pencil tests. Already many foreign language tests are at least partially on audio tapes. An area that will receive intense interest will be computer-based testing. The advantages of using the computer as tester are several and obvious: greater uniformity of testing conditions, flexibility in order of presentation of items, automatic recording and scoring of responses, and immediate feedback to the test taker.

There will be more questioning of the value and function of tests. Rather than uncritically adopting a testing program, there will be greater demands to justify the use of tests, to show that the

---

[2] As the average ability of students will vary between schools, one must adjust test usage accordingly. Suppose an achievement test is published with overlapping levels—e.g., grades 2–4 and 4–7. A school in an upper middle-class neighborhood might elect to use the higher level (4–7) to test their fourth-grade students, while an inner-city school might feel the lower level (2–4) was more appropriate for their fourth-grade students.

tests will provide useful information. While this questioning will be particularly directed toward personality measures (where the issue of invasion of privacy is raised) and in selection situations (where the issue of possible biases obtains), it will probably spread to all areas of testing. If the questioning remains on a rational and constructive level, it will serve to improve the quality of tests and test usage; irrational diatribes, however, will advance neither testing nor the educational process.

We are also witnessing an increasing emphasis on mastery testing and attempts to develop criterion-referenced scores. Rather than using tests solely to measure differences between individuals, we are also asking if tests aid in ascertaining whether students have mastered the objectives of instruction. In other words, there will be less emphasis on "who knows more than whom" and more emphasis on "what students do and do not know."

The emphasis of mastery testing can be subsumed under our final point, that there will be more integration between testing and instruction. Tests will be seen as aids to make decisions about the sequence of educational experiences which will be optimal for an individual student and as tools used to evaluate the effectiveness of educational programs. These evaluations may be quite specific, confined to a given unit or microunit of instruction, or very broad, such as the National Assessment or the International Study of Achievement in Mathematics. Thus test use will focus on questions such as: What are we trying to teach? How effective was our teaching? What is the relationship between particular student characteristics and the optimal sequence of educational experiences?

That there has not previously been a closer integration of testing and instruction is the result of many factors. But the present trend is to be applauded. For if tests do not aid in planning educational experiences for individual students or help evaluate the effects of instructional materials and methods, they would seem to have little value in the educational process.

APPENDIX A. STATISTICAL CONCEPTS

A knowledge of several basic statistical concepts is necessary in order to understand certain concepts in testing. For example, one cannot clearly understand the concepts of reliability and criterion-related validity without knowing what is meant by correlation, nor can standard scores be fully understood without knowledge of the standard deviation. Thus some knowledge of elementary statistics is necessary in order to comprehend parts of this book.

As most readers will have had only minimal exposure to statistics, we have kept statistical concepts to a minimum. When statistical concepts were introduced, the emphasis was on understanding the basic concept rather than technical details or computational methods. In addition, this appendix briefly summarizes the statistics used in the text. It may be studied as a separate unit or used as a reference.

Although we will illustrate computational procedures, the purpose of the examples is primarily to facilitate understanding of the concepts, and only secondarily to teach computational procedures. Thus we have used simple examples; the student who wishes to develop more skill in this area should take a course in educational or psychological statistics.

Descriptive Statistics

The statistics discussed are all descriptive; that is, they summarize and describe a set of data. We will discuss three types of measures: central tendency, variability, and correlation. Measures of central tendency summarize the average score of a set of data in one index. Measures of variability indicate the dispersion within a set of scores—how widely the scores vary. Correlation is a measure of the relationship between two sets of scores obtained from the same sample of persons. Although many other indices and types of statistics are utilized in test development and research, the simple indices discussed below are sufficient for comprehension of the materials in this book.

Central Tendency

A single number which represents the average performance of the entire set of scores is often a useful index. Three such indices are in common use—the mode, the median, and the mean.

The *mode* is the score which occurs most frequently. Although the mode is a very rough index, being based on only one score, it will be sufficient if a large proportion of the group obtains one particular score. For example, if we wanted to know the average age at which children enter kindergarten, the mode would be a sufficient index, as the majority of students entering kindergarten would be the same age, five years old.

The *median* can be defined as the score above and below which 50 percent of the scores fall. To compute the median, arrange the scores in order of magnitude and find the score value that divides the group into halves. The median is particularly useful when there are several atypically high or low scores or when the distribution of scores is skewed (i.e., more scores fall towards one end of the distribution; see Figure 5.2).

The most useful measure of central tendency is the arithmetic average, or *mean*. The mean is calculated by summing all the scores and dividing by the number of scores:

$$\bar{X} = \frac{\Sigma X}{n} \qquad \text{(A.1)}$$

where $\bar{X}$ is the symbol for the mean, X is an individual score, Σ means "the sum of," and n is the number of scores summed.

An example will clarify. A teacher gives a quiz and prepares a *frequency distribution* showing the number of students (the frequency, f) who receive each score (X):

Score (X)	15	14	13	12	11	10	9	8	7	6	5	4	3	2	1
Frequency (f)	1	3	2	3	4	7	10	6	4	2	3	2	1	2	0

To compute the mean we first sum all the scores. This sum can be obtained by multiplying each score (X_i) by its frequency (f_i) and summing over all scores:

$$\Sigma X = \Sigma X_i f_i, \text{ or}$$
$$\Sigma X = (15)(1) + (14)(3) + (13)(2) + \cdots + (2)(2) = 441$$

Then divide by the number of scores:

$$\overline{X} = \frac{\Sigma X}{n} = \frac{441}{50} = 8.82 \text{ or } 8.8$$

This value, 8.8, is the average score, or mean, for this set of scores.

Variability

As with central tendency, there are several possible measures of variability. However, the most useful measure is the *standard deviation*, which can be defined:

$$s = \sqrt{\frac{\Sigma x^2}{n}} \qquad\qquad (A.2)$$

Formula A.2 says that the standard deviation (s) is the square root of the average squared deviation from the mean, where a deviation (x) score is the difference between a score and the mean $(x = X - \overline{X})$.

The interpretation of the standard deviation will be discussed below. But, first, we will calculate s for our set of scores. There are several ways of proceeding. Using formula A.2, we would first find for every score:

> when $X = 15$, $x = 15 - 8.8 = 6.2$
> when $X = 14$, $x = 14 - 8.8 = 5.2$, and so on through
> when $X = 2$, $x = 2 - 8.8 = -6.8$

We would then compute Σx^2 by squaring each x, multiplying by the number of times the score occurred, and summing:

$$\Sigma x^2 = (6.2)^2(1) + (5.2)^2(3) + \ldots + (-6.8)^2(2) = 463.4$$

Then substituting in formula A.2:

$$s = \sqrt{\frac{\Sigma x^2}{n}} = \sqrt{\frac{463.4}{50}} = 3.04 \text{ or } 3.0$$

(We could also obtain the same result using a raw score formula:

$$s = \frac{1}{n} \sqrt{n\Sigma X^2 - (\Sigma X)^2} \qquad \text{(A.2a)}$$

The interested student can confirm this by performing the calculations.)

We should also note that another index of variability, the square of the standard deviation (s^2), which is called the *variance*, is a very useful statistic. Its usefulness derives from the fact that the various components contributing to variance can be analyzed and the proportion of variance attributable to each factor determined.

The interpretation of the standard deviation is based on the fact that, when scores approach a normal distribution, definite percentages of scores fall within certain standard deviation limits of the mean (see figure below):

These relationships provide a basis for interpreting scores: for example, 68 percent of the scores will fall within (plus or minus) one standard deviation of the mean, almost all scores fall within ± 3s of the mean, only 16 percent of the scores fall higher than + 1s. (These relations are also the basis of standard scores; see Chapter 3.)

Correlation

The measures discussed above apply when there is only one score for each individual. However, in many situations we are interested in comparing two sets of data obtained from the same group of persons. Examples include determining the relationship between students' scores on two exams, between students' grades in two classes, between scores on an aptitude test and a measure of achievement, between teachers' estimates of students' ability and their test scores, and so on. In these instances we want an index of the degree to which scores will rank in the same relative positions on the two measures. Technically, we want to know the correlation

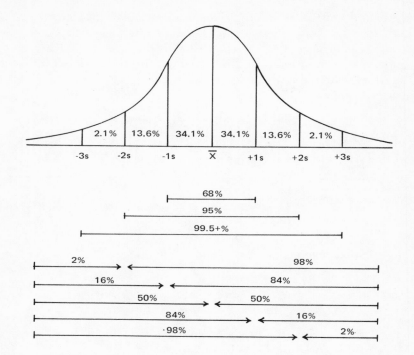

(literally co-relation) between the two sets of scores. Although various measures of correlation are available, the one most commonly used in educational measurement is the Pearson product-moment correlation coefficient (r).

The value of r can range from $+1.00$ through 0.00 to -1.00. The magnitude of the coefficient indicates how closely the two sets of scores are related. Thus a perfect correlation ($r = 1.00$) indicates that corresponding scores in the two sets rank in the same relative positions. Stated differently, when $r = 1.00$, knowing a student's score on one variable allows us to predict with perfect accuracy his score on the other. (Of course, we almost never attain this degree of correspondence.) The farther r departs from unity (i.e., the closer it approaches zero), the less correspondence in ranking and the less accurately we can predict one variable from the other. Thus, $r = .23$ indicates a lower degree of correspondence (predictability) than does $r = .73$.

The correlation coefficient can have either a positive or a negative sign. A positive sign indicates that high scores on one variable are associated with high scores on the other, and low scores are associated with low scores. Negative correlations indicate that high scores on one variable are associated with low scores on the other. Scatterplots showing the distribution of scores with varying degrees of correlation are shown below (the shaded area indicates the distribution of pairs of scores):

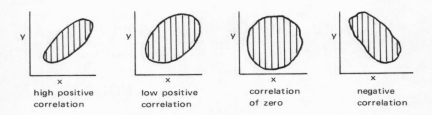

| high positive correlation | low positive correlation | correlation of zero | negative correlation |

The correlation coefficient is usually defined as:

$$r = \frac{\Sigma xy}{ns_x s_y} = \frac{\Sigma z_x z_y}{n} \qquad (A.3)$$

where $z = x/s$ and the other terms have previously been defined. More useful computational formulae are:

$$r = \frac{\Sigma XY/n - (\bar{X})(\bar{Y})}{s_x s_y} \text{ and} \qquad (A.3a)$$

$$r = \frac{N\Sigma XY - (\Sigma X)(\Sigma Y)}{\sqrt{N\Sigma X^2 - (\Sigma X)^2} \sqrt{N\Sigma Y^2 - (\Sigma Y)^2}} \qquad (A.3b)$$

where all terms have been previously defined. To illustrate the computation of a correlation coefficient, assume that 10 students took two tests, with results as follows:

Student	A	B	C	D	E	F	G	H	I	J	$\bar{X}$	s
Test X	10	9	8	7	7	7	6	6	5	4	6.9	1.7
Test Y	8	9	8	5	7	6	4	7	5	6	6.5	1.5

Using formula A.3a, we first find the sum of the cross-products (ΣXY) by multiplying each person's (two) scores together, then summing across all individuals:

$$\Sigma XY = (10)(8) + (9)(9) + (8)(8) + \ldots + (4)(6) = 466$$

Then substituting into formula A.3a:

$$r = \frac{466/10 - (6.9)(6.5)}{(1.7)(1.5)} = .69$$

(The reader, as an exercise, can compute r using an alternative procedure.)

To interpret a correlation coefficient is somewhat difficult. One common way is in terms of variance (see above). It can be shown that the square of the correlation coefficient (r^2) indicates the proportion of variance the two measures have in common. In our example $r^2 = (.69)^2 = .48$; thus we can say that 48 percent of the variability in scores is attributable to factors common to both, while the remaining 52 percent is attributable to factors specific to each test.

This leads to one final point about correlation. A correlation coefficient only indicates degree of relationship; it does not indicate causation. If variables X and Y are correlated, this could mean that (1) X causes variation in Y, (2) Y causes the variation in X, or (3) the variation in both X and Y is caused by a third factor common to both X and Y. To illustrate, if we find a correlation between scores on a vocabulary test and on a measure of reading comprehension, we do not know whether the proper interpretation is that (1) possession of a good vocabulary increases reading comprehension, or (2) being able to read with high comprehension increases one's vocabulary, or (3) reading comprehension and vocabulary are both dependent on some other ability.

APPENDIX B. EXAMPLES OF STANDARDIZED TESTS

ACHIEVEMENT BATTERIES

California Achievement Tests (California Test Bureau). Five levels (grades 1–2, 2–4, 4–6, 7–9, 9–14); equivalent forms; 1½–3 hours. Measures Reading (vocabulary, comprehension), Arithmetic (reasoning, fundamentals) and Language (mechanics, spelling). Measures educational attainment and diagnoses learning difficulties in basic skills.

Comprehensive Tests of Basic Skills (California Test Bureau). Four levels (2.5–4, 4–6, 6–8, 8–12); equivalent forms; 3+ hours. Reading (vocabulary, comprehension), Language (mechanics, expression, spelling), Arithmetic (concepts, computations, applications), Study Skills (reference materials, graphic materials). Emphasis on basic concepts, relations, skills.

Iowa Tests of Basic Skills (Houghton Mifflin). Grades 3–9; equivalent forms; 6+ hours. Vocabulary, Reading Comprehension, Language (spelling, capitalization, punctuation, usage), Work-Study Skills (graphs, reference materials, tables, maps), Arithmetic Skills (concepts, problem solving). Uses generalized skills approach.

Iowa Tests of Educational Development (Science Research Associates). Grades 9–12; equivalent forms; 2 days. Understanding of basic social concepts, Background in the natural sciences, Correctness and appropriateness of expression, Ability to do quantitative thinking, Ability to interpret reading materials in social sciences, Ability to interpret reading materials in natural sciences, Ability to interpret literary materials, General vocabulary, Uses of sources of information. Measures broad and generalized intellectual skills and abilities; what student can do, not what he knows.

Metropolitan Achievement Tests (Harcourt, Brace & World). Six levels (1, 2, 3–4, 5–6, 7–9, high school 9–13); equivalent forms; 2–4 hours. Content varies by level: Primary II (grade 2) tests Word Knowledge, Word Discrimination, Reading, Spelling, Arithmetic Concepts and Skills; Intermediate (5–6) covers Word Knowledge, Reading, Spelling, Language, Language Study Skills, Arithmetic Computation, Arithmetic Problem Solving and Concepts, Social Studies Information, Social Studies Study Skills, Science. Concepts and information tested separately.

SRA Achievement Series (Science Research Associates). Four levels (1–2, 2–4, 3–4, 4–9 multilevel); equivalent forms. Content varies by level: Multilevel (4–9) covers Reading (vocabulary, comprehension), Arithmetic (reasoning, concepts, computations), Language Arts (capitalization and punctuation, grammar usage, spelling), Social Studies, Science, Work-Study Skills (optional). Also has an optional test of modern math understanding.

Sequential Tests of Educational Progress (Cooperative Tests Division, Educational Testing Service). Four levels (4–6, 7–9, 10–12, 13–14); equivalent forms; 70 minutes per test. Reading, Writing, Listening (questions on orally presented materials), Mathematics, Science, Social Studies.

Stanford Achievement Test (Harcourt, Brace & World). Six levels (1.5–2.4, 2.5–3.9, 4.0–5.9, 5.5–6.9, 7.0–9.9, high school); equivalent forms; up to 5+ hours. Coverage varies by level: Reading (word meaning, paragraph meaning), Language Arts, Arithmetic (computations, concepts) appear at all levels; Science and Social Studies from grade 4 up; other tests at various levels.

SCHOLASTIC APTITUDE TESTS

California Test of Mental Maturity (California Test Bureau). Kindergarten–college; long form—6 levels, short form—8 levels; provides Language, Nonlanguage and Total scale scores; patterned after the Binet.

Differential Aptitude Tests (The Psychological Corporation). Grades 8–12; the combined score on two sections, Verbal Reasoning + Numerical Ability, is used as an index of scholastic aptitude.

Henmon-Nelson Tests of Mental Ability (Houghton Mifflin). Grades 3–college; 4 levels; Verbal, Quantitative, and Total scores; items arranged in omnibus cycle by difficulty.

Kuhlmann-Anderson Measure of Academic Potential (The Psychological Corporation). Kindergarten–college freshmen; 8 levels; Verbal, Quantitative, and Total scores for grade 7 and up.

Lorge-Thorndike Intelligence Tests (Houghton Mifflin). Kindergarten–college; 6 levels; Verbal and Nonverbal scores from grade 4 up, only Nonverbal below grade 4.

Ohio State University Psychological Examination (W. L. Layton). Grades 9–college; vocabulary, analogies, and reading comprehension; untimed; short form, The Minnesota Scholastic Aptitude Test, also available.

Otis-Lennon Mental Ability Test (Harcourt, Brace & World). Kindergarten–12; 6 levels; one total score; mental ages available at primary and elementary levels.

School and College Ability Tests (Cooperative Test Division, Educational Testing Service). Grade 4–college; 4 levels; Verbal, Mathematical and Total scores.

Short Tests of Educational Ability (Science Research Associates). Kindergarten–12; 5 levels; grades K-3 use only pictorial materials.

Tests of Educational Ability (Science Research Associates). Grades 4–12; 3 levels; measures Language, Reasoning, and Quantitative skills.

COLLEGE ADMISSIONS TESTS

American College Testing program (ACT). Four subtests, 40–50 minutes each—English Usage, Mathematical Usage, Social Studies, Reading, Natural Sciences Reading—plus Composite score (average of subtests scores); emphasis on developed skills; constant revision.

Scholastic Aptitude Test (College Entrance Examination Board). Verbal (e.g., word relations and meaning, reading comprehension) and Mathematical (understanding and reasoning with mathematical symbols) sections; 3 hours; constant revision; battery also includes a series of achievement test in specific subjects.

INDEX

[Italicized page numbers refer to citation at the end of the chapters.]

Logical error, 147
Lorge-Thorndike Intelligence Test, 121–126, 192
Lyman, H. B., 31, *46*

Mager, R. F., 13, *27, 49, 73*
Magnusson, D., 17, *27*
Marking (*see* Grading)
Marshall, M. S., 153, *159*
Mastery testing, 4, 90–92
Matching items, 60–61
Mathematics, International Study of Achievement in, 172
Maximal performance tests, 15
McNemar, Q., 132, *139*
Mean, 81, 184–185
Measurement, defined, 9–10
  scales, 9
  versus evaluation, 10
  versus learning, 10
Median, 80–81, 184
Meehl, P. E., 24, *27*
Mehrens, W. A., 1, *11*, 100, *114*, 122, 137, *139*
Mental age, 36, 119
Mental Measurements Yearbooks, 137
Merrill, M., 117
Merwin, J. C., 91, *93*, 168, *176*
Metropolitan Achievement Tests, 191
Minnesota Vocational Interest Inventory, 136
Minority groups, testing of, 96–97, 113, 133–134
Modal age grade norms, 107
Mode, 80, 184
Motivation, as a function of tests, 48–49
  grades as motivators, 142
Multiple aptitude test batteries, 126–128
Multiple-choice items, 56–58
  guidelines for writing, 58

National Assessment of Educational Progress, 91, 168
Normal distribution, 78–80
Normal percentile chart, 39–40
Normalized standard scores, 34
Norm-referenced scores, 41

Norms and normative data, 28–30, 37–41
  desired characteristics of, 28–30
  local norms, 30
  methods of presenting, 37–41
  on standardized achievement tests, 96–97, 106–107
Numerical rating scales, 145–146

Objectives, instructional, 13–14
  role in test planning, 49–51
Ohio State University Psychological Examination, 192
Ordinal scale, 9
Otis–Lennon Mental Ability Test, 192
Outputs, educational, 164–165

Pace, C. R., 169, *176*
Panos, R. J., 161, 162, 163, 165, 166, *175*
Pass-fail grading systems, 158
Percentage scale (score), 31
  in grading, 151–152
Percentiles, 31, 33
  percentile points, 31
  percentile ranks, 31
  percentile ranks within grades, 36, 106–107
  use in grading, 148–149
Performance items, 55, 70
Performance rating (*see* Rating)
Personality measurement, 135–137
Placement, 2–7
Planning, classroom tests, 49–54
  test plans, 50–53
Popham, W. J., 42, *46*
Power tests, 15
Practical considerations in test selection, 25–26
Prediction, of academic success, 133–134
  predictive validity, 22–23
Problem items, 55, 69
Profiles, test, 39–40
Projective methods, 136

Quasi-experiments, 163

Rating scales, 145–148
  methods, 145–147
  rating errors, 147

Ratio IQ, 36
Ratio scores, 36–37
Raw scores, 30–31
Readiness tests, 104–105
Reliability, 16–21
  coefficients, 17–19
  computation of, 82–83
  of standardized achievement
    tests, 105–106
  role in score interpretation, 43
Rosenthal, R., 133, *139*

Sanford, N., 170, *176*
Scholastic Aptitude Test (SAT),
  43–44, 122, 192
Scholastic aptitude tests, 120–126,
  191–192
*School and College Ability Tests
  (SCAT)*, 192
School testing programs, 179–181
*Science Research Associates (SRA)
  Achievement Series*, 191
Scores, 30–45
  age, 34–35
  analysis of, 77–85
  combining, 154–156
  content, 41–42
  criterion-referenced, 41–42
  derived, 31–37
  developmental, 34–36
  deviation IQ, 36
  distributions of, 77–80
  equating, 43–44
  error of measurement in, 43
  expectancy tables, 39–41
  grade, 35–36
  intelligence quotient (IQ), 36,
    119–120
  interpretation of, 42–45
  meaning of, summarized, 177–
    178
  mental age, 36
  methods of presenting, 37–41
  normal percentiles, 39–40
  normalized standard scores, 34
  norm-referenced, 41
  percentage, 31
  percentile points, 31
  percentile ranks, 31
  percentile ranks within grades, 36
  profiles, 39–40

Scores (*Continued*)
  ratio, 36–37
  ratio IQ, 36
  raw, 30–31
  standard scores, 32–34
  stanines, 34
  transformed, 31–37
  z, 32–34
  Z, 32–34
Scoring, 16, 74–77
  correction for guessing, 75–76
  essay questions, 76
  keys, 16, 75
  weights, 77
Seashore, H. G., 33, 38, 40
Self-report inventories, 135–136
*Sequential Tests of Educational
  Progress (STEP)*, 191
Severity error, 147
Short-answer items, 61–65
  defined, 55
  guidelines for writing, 63
Short Tests of Educational Ability,
  192
Situational methods, 136
Skewed distribution, 79–80
Skinner, B. F., 49, *73*
Smith, A. Z., 140, *159*
Specimen set, 137
Speed test, 15
Split-half reliability, 19
  computation of, 82–83
Stability, coefficient of, 17–18
Stability and equivalence, coefficient
  of, 18
Standard deviation, 81–82, 185–186
Standard error of measurement, 21
Standard scale rating, 146
Standard scores, 32–34
  use in grading, 150–151
Standardized tests, 47–48, 95–139
  of achievement, 95–114, 190–191
  of intellectual ability, 115–134,
    191–192
Standardization, 12–16
Stanford Achievement Test Series,
  98–104, 191
Stanford-Binet Intelligence Scale,
  117–119
Stanines, 34
Stanley, J. C., 163, 166, *175*

Measurement and Evaluation was typeset, printed by offset and bound at Kingsport Press, Inc. The paper is Perkins & Squier Company's Glatfelter Old Forge. Internal and cover design was by Charles Kling & Associates. The type in this book is Caledonia with Helvetica display.